"Courtney Ellis tells the truth about par⟨
the joys and the chaos is an opportunity
experiment with practicing the classic sp
diapers, and managing bedtime, and yo⟨ ⟩⟨⟩⟩⟨⟩⟨⟩⟩⟨ ⟩⟨ ⟩⟩⟨⟩⟨⟩⟩⟨⟩⟩⟨ ⟩⟨ ⟩⟩⟨ ⟩⟩⟨ ⟩⟨⟩⟩⟨⟩

—**Catherine McNiel**, author of *Long Days of Small Things:
Motherhood as a Spiritual Discipline*

"*Almost Holy Mama* is an encouraging guide for parents who want to draw close
to Jesus during one of life's busiest and most exhausting seasons. From pregnancy
to the school years and beyond, Courtney Ellis offers a thoughtful, hilarious guide
to finding Jesus amongst a particularly messy—and deeply joyful—time of life."

—**Jana Alayra**, singer, songwriter, and worship leader

"Combining good humor with deep, practical wisdom, *Almost Holy Mama* is a
rare accomplishment. Courtney Ellis comes alongside us as both the mentor that
we weary parents long for and the friend that we need."

—**Chris Blumhofer**, visiting assistant professor at Fuller Seminary

"With wit and honesty, Courtney Ellis shares her story of learning to weave
disciplines like prayer, fasting, contemplation, and service into the warp and woof
of her days parenting small children. Her confessional style and practical, wise
insight show parents of young children how to practice the presence of God in the
car, in the shower, folding laundry, or through months of morning sickness. She is
a relatable guide to your Lego-strewn journey with Jesus through the challenging
early years of parenting."

—**Michelle Van Loon**, author of *Born to Wander: Recovering
the Value of Our Pilgrim Identity*

"Courtney Ellis is that warm, funny friend who will look you in the eye and point
you to Jesus. Walk through the church year and spiritual disciplines with her;
practice contemplation, confession, and stillness in your minivan, and you'll see
how 'busy and tired' is the entrance for God to work. *Almost Holy Mama* is full of
grace, humor, and a relentless desire to grow in holiness—not to prove ourselves
to God but to learn again how to live as little children. It's a message we all need."

—**Ashley Hales**, author of *Finding Holy in the Suburbs: Living
Faithfully in the Land of Too Much*

"With wit and vulnerability, Courtney Ellis permits her readers access to the
distinctive challenges and joys she encounters as a mother, a minister, and an
everyday disciple of Jesus. By combining the playfulness of Anne Lamott with the
spiritual earnestness of a Eugene Peterson or James K. A. Smith, Ellis reminds us
of two things simultaneously: that the spiritual disciplines are serious business, and
that there's no reason we can't have a holy sense of humor about our occasionally
stumbling attempts to practice them."

—**Kevin McLenithan**, film critic, and cohost of the *Seeing and
Believing* podcast

"It turns out that to effectively practice classic spiritual disciplines you don't have to have taken vows and live in a monastery or a convent. Courtney Ellis gives us a graceful glimpse into how these Christian disciplines can find a place in our twenty-first-century, everyday lives. It's a practical, rich, insightful guide."

—**Shawn Smucker**, author of *Once We Were Strangers: What Friendship with a Syrian Refugee Taught Me about Loving My Neighbor*

"[Courtney Ellis] shows us with clarity, humor, and tons of #reallife examples what it is like to be present—to yourself, to your children, to your partner, and to God's presence all around. This book is what tired mamas like me have been looking for: how we find God in the lives we inhabit (not the ones we used to have or might have ten years from now). I can't wait to share this book with my congregation and mom friends."

—**Elizabeth Hagan**, author of *Birthed: Finding Grace through Infertility*, and senior minister of Palisades Community Church

"For those of us called to both parent children and deepen our faith, simply making it through the day can be exhausting, much less days spent trying to be present with God and family. With *Almost Holy Mama*, Courtney Ellis has written a practical and feasible (not easy, thank God!) guide to maintaining an intentionally close walk with God without giving up your relationship with your family—and vice versa. I laughed at some chapters, winced at others, and have already made plans to integrate some of these disciplines into my family's life. What a gift this book is for parents, for families, and for the churches they belong to."

—**Ryan Hamm**, senior writer at Open Doors USA, former managing editor of *RELEVANT* magazine

"If you're anything like me, the pursuit of holiness can get lost in the shuffle of work, laundry, meal prep, kids' activities, and school demands. In *Almost Holy Mama*, Courtney Ellis offers hope for the always overextended mom to forge a deeper relationship with God in what may seem to be unlikely places, from the carpool lane to the shower to the playground. I'm grateful to be reminded that I don't have to be a monastic to access holiness because God is more than willing to meet me in the midst of my crazy-busy, sometimes overwhelming, but beautiful family life."

—**Harmony Harkema**, writer, editor, speaker, and writing coach

"In *Almost Holy Mama*, Courtney Ellis invites us with wit, compassion, and wisdom toward practices that move us closer to the awareness of God with us. Readers will find Courtney to be an honest and trustworthy guide as she embraces various spiritual practices, and works to integrate them into her full life as a mom and a minister. This book will inevitably make you laugh, but also practically consider the ways God is calling us in everyday moments toward greater connection with him."

—**Aundi Kolber**, therapist, speaker, and author

almost
holy
mama

LIFE-GIVING SPIRITUAL PRACTICES
FOR WEARY PARENTS

COURTNEY ELLIS

To Lauren —
Peace in the parenting journey ♡
Courtney Ellis

HENDRICKSON PUBLISHERS   ROSE PUBLISHING

Almost Holy Mama
Rose Publishing, LLC
140 Summit Street
P.O. Box 3473
Peabody, Massachusetts 01961-3473
www.hendricksonrose.com

All Scripture quotations, unless otherwise indicated, are taken from the Holy Bible, New International Version®, NIV®. Copyright ©1973, 1978, 1984, 2011 by Biblica, Inc.™ Used by permission of Zondervan. All rights reserved worldwide. www.zondervan.com The "NIV" and "New International Version" are trademarks registered in the United States Patent and Trademark Office by Biblica, Inc.™

Scripture quotations marked (ESV) are from the ESV® Bible (The Holy Bible, English Standard Version®), copyright © 2001 by Crossway, a publishing ministry of Good News Publishers. Used by permission. All rights reserved.

Scripture quotations marked (RSV) are from the Revised Standard Version of the Bible, copyright © 1946, 1952, and 1971 National Council of the Churches of Christ in the United States of America. Used by permission. All rights reserved worldwide.

Scripture quotations marked (NKJV) are taken from the New King James Version®. Copyright © 1982 by Thomas Nelson. Used by permission. All rights reserved.

Scripture quotations marked (NLT) are taken from the Holy Bible, New Living Translation, copyright ©1996, 2004, 2015 by Tyndale House Foundation. Used by permission of Tyndale House Publishers, Inc., Carol Stream, Illinois 60188. All rights reserved.

Scripture quotations marked MSG are taken from THE MESSAGE, copyright © 1993, 1994, 1995, 1996, 2000, 2001, 2002 by Eugene H. Peterson. Used by permission of NavPress. All rights reserved. Represented by Tyndale House Publishers, Inc.

Book cover design by Nancy Bishop; page design by Nancy Bishop and Sergio Urquiza.

ISBN: 978-1-62862-790-9

Printed in the United States of America

010319VP

To Lincoln, Wilson, and Felicity,
I love you to the moon

Being made holy is not a one-time deal;
it's an ongoing process.
… The key idea to remember is that we pass
"through" and do not remain in the fire.
—Enuma Okoro

TABLE OF CONTENTS

FOREWORD

Like millions of brave women who came before me, I spent the first several months of my second pregnancy throwing my guts up. My then-toddler is now a ten-year-old with an uncanny ability to remember all my worst moments from his early childhood, including one from that season when we walked to the bank from our small apartment in urban San Francisco, hand in hand.

"Honey," I said to my toddler as dozens of errand runners and tourists shuffled past us, "Let's sit right here." I was pointing to a portion of sidewalk beside a building, between two garbage bins. "Mommy feels kind of bad." The truth is that I didn't get the word *bad* out before slumping onto hands and knees, shaking, and searching my bag for the yogurt squeeze pouch that sometimes quelled my early pregnancy nausea, holding my son's hand all the while.

It was so long ago, of course, and I have all sorts of memories of my second pregnancy (like when my son followed me in tears to the bathroom and angrily closed the toilet lid on my head while I vomited). But *this* is the moment he remembers. In my memory I held it together. In *his* memory, I threw up while he watched, along with all the strangers who walked past us.

The truth is that our story of motherhood is always also our child's story. We have no control over what they receive and hold tight to. My son and I walked to the bank fairly often in those days. We usually paused at the big trees at Washington Square Park and stopped by the Italian espresso bar on Columbus Ave. He doesn't remember any of that. What he remembers never actually happened: my vomiting on the sidewalk between the garbage bins.

Maybe that's a metaphor for motherhood, how little control we have over what sticks, who our kids become and what ultimately forms them. The longer I've been a mother the more I've become convinced I can control little beyond one thing: my willingness to invite God to form me.

Raising my babies has been a long, slow, dangerous journey up a cliff face. The rocks that tear my hands have also made them strong. And each time I feel capable, the terrain changes, forcing me to learn a new way forward. We build muscles for nursery rhymes and boo-boo kisses; then realize our kids are preteens who need us to walk them through the dangers of porn on the internet. We're fumbling, all of us.

God's invitation in parenting is grace, magic we discover in the midst of struggle, in the disorientation of continuous change. Grace shows up when I'm brave enough to look over my shoulder, when I see a vision of sky that can only be glimpsed from the height I'm climbing. It's stuns me and awakens me to a reality I never before knew was true. Grace is everywhere, if we learn to look over our shoulders.

There is a way to make it up the side of the cliff with joy, with delight, despite the exhaustion and desperate chaos of daily life with small kids. We find that strength of joy by practicing the spiritual work of turning around.

Almost Holy Mama is a book about that kind of looking. The gift of Courtney's story is how she takes the lonely, ordinary moments of motherhood—midnight songs in the rocking chair, laundry folding, saving the child from toppling off the seesaw—and holds them up to the light. She reminds us that all the moments have value, and that Jesus sees them even when no one else does. "The God we serve," she says, "is never far off; he enters into our perceived monotony, the daily rhythms of our lives, in order to make something extraordinary out of it all. Out of us."

Courtney recognizes that in the middle of those chaotic early years of motherhood our need for the presence of Jesus is fierce. Her story is a light for the long days of repetition and anxiety. She reminds us that, yes, there is time and space to be with Jesus. Sometimes it's in the car with two toddlers buckled into car seats behind us. Sometimes it's during bedtime rituals with our little ones. And sometimes we find Jesus in the laundry, in the shower, in our own suffering.

She reminds us that we are held in grace. The climb is dangerous and sometimes overwhelming, but grace is extraordinary, and the view shines bright with the magic of God.

I'm grateful for the reminder.

Micha Boyett
Epiphany, 2019

CHAPTER 1

RUNNING ON EMPTY, LONGING FOR MORE

Peace must be dared.
—Dietrich Bonhoeffer

"Why aren't you cranky right now?" I asked my sister Caitlyn as she patiently wrestled her squirmy second-born into a fresh diaper. "You woke up before 5 a.m. and you're up to your wrists in poop. *I'd* be cranky."

"Coffee," she said. She held her daughter down gently with one hand while pulling more wipes out of the box with the other.

"Seriously, Cait, I am tired just watching you. Did you sleep at all last night?" I hadn't yet learned that asking mothers of newborns this particular question was unhelpful at best. The answer is almost always *no*; better not to dwell on it. (I also obviously hadn't learned that commentary is far less helpful than *help*. What kind of sister sits idly by without at least handing over a few wipes?) Cait fastened the snaps on Sophia's flowered fleece pajamas and picked her up.

"Well, I'm not going to let her *sit* there in it," she said, shrugging. "I love her, and she needed a fresh diaper."

"Your sister is holier than we are," my husband whispered to me. We didn't have kids of our own yet, and we weren't in any hurry. Parenting looked *hard*.

Now, nearly seven years later, we have two growing boys of our own—a toddler and a kindergartener—and we await the arrival of our youngest, a baby girl, in just a few weeks. This parenting thing? It *is* hard. So hard. Good and holy and beautiful? Yes. Sacred and meaningful and a privilege? Of course. But *hard*. I've run a marathon, walked for months on a broken ankle, and moaned my way through natural childbirth twice, and in comparison to the daily grind of parenting, all those were *cake*.

Every parent has come to the end of his or her rope more than once. Those of us who are honest will admit it's more like once a day (or an hour…). We struggle mightily to get out of bed for another midnight feeding; we change a couple thousand diapers every year. We may think if we have to pack *one more freaking snack* we are going to *lose* it. We come to the end of ourselves regularly and often. But here's the thing: we pack the snack anyway. We get out of bed anyway. We change the diaper anyway. We've all been out of our depth, overwhelmed, and exhausted (probably even today), but somehow, some way, we keep going…because these small people depend on us, and God has entrusted them to our care. But it's not easy. Oh boy, is it *not* easy.

Raising kids is relentless work. There's joy, too—lots of it— but when the sink is piled high with dishes, the infant is teething, the grade schooler keeps singing the same five bars of "Home on the Range," you're fighting a stomach bug, and the whole household is running late *again*, joyful feelings can seem tauntingly elusive. My friend Beth calls parenting "the only job you'll be consistently and completely terrible at, but can't quit." Preach.

Yet between the throes of exhaustion and the profound joys that come with parenting, many of us find ourselves longing for something deeper. Something more. You might remember the closeness you felt to Jesus in years past, back in high school or college or when you were first married or before you landed that full-time job that turned out to require eighty hours a week—back when you had *time* to give to God. Or maybe you've never really had a relationship with God before, not in any sort of established or consistent way, but you sense there's something missing in your life. You long for depth, for connection, for your spirit to unite with something richer and more lasting than the ephemeral everyday.

As I searched for help, for ways to draw closer to Jesus in the intense crucible that is parenthood, I discovered two things:

First, there *is* a proven way to commune with Jesus and integrate the love of God into daily life. (The gospel really is good news, folks!) That way is time-tested and almost universally accepted throughout Christendom, whether you're Roman Catholic, marginally Methodist, or decidedly nondenominational. This path is the journey of spiritual disciplines: soul-care practices like prayer and fasting, solitude and silence, worship and community. Each of these is a biblical, time-honored, ancient way to open our hearts to the things of God.

The bad news came second, as I quickly discovered that the bulk of the writings on spiritual practices comes from priests, monks, and nuns, each of whom lacks every parent's primary personal concern: children. Other great guides came from men who primarily worked outside the home. Even modern classics like Richard Foster's *A Celebration of Discipline* and Eugene Peterson's *A Long Obedience in the Same Direction* (both of which have been quite formative in my own life) were written by men who served as pastors and academics, not primary caregivers to young kids. Each of these people, to one degree or another, had what every caregiving parent is in extremely short supply of: *time*.

George MacDonald could encourage me to pray for two hours every morning and Teresa of Avila could plead with me to retreat in solitude to be with Jesus, but I was all *YOU DON'T KNOW MY LIFE*. If I spent two hours in prayer every morning, I'd have to get up at 3 a.m., and even then, it would be interrupted by at least one nursing session and seventeen requests for juice. If I retreated in solitude to be with Jesus, my kids would either starve to death or burn our house to the ground. (Look, Mommy! I can turn the oven on!)

Over and over again in Scripture we read of Jesus—our definitive model for what it is to be human and what it looks like to be in faithful relationship to the Father—withdrawing to a quiet place to pray. He goes up on a mountain. He takes a boat out away from the crowds. He sits in a garden. I rarely get to do any of that. If I was going up a mountain, I'd have an alternately hungry and poopy baby in a carrier on my back. If I took a boat out, I'd spend all my time making sure everyone had a proper personal flotation device and no one hung too far out over the side. If I was sitting in a garden, I'd be answering a thousand of my older son's questions about what that flower was, why the snail was hiding in its shell, and how come he couldn't pour dirt down my shirt. *Quiet places* indeed.

There seemed to be only two real options for practicing spiritual disciplines as a parent:

1) **It was impossible**—at least until the kids either went to school full-time or graduated and moved out.

2) **It was possible** if I just tried harder.

The first option *couldn't* be true. I don't believe in a God who sets us up for failure or holds out spiritual gifts that will only be attainable if we head to a nunnery. God is *intensely* practical and interested in the ordinary, everyday, mundane elements of our lives. It's why he chooses bread and wine to represent his body and blood in the sacrament of Communion, and plain old water for holy baptism. It's why he came down from his heavenly throne to take on flesh—skin and bones and lungs and teeth—to live among us in the person of Jesus. God loves the ordinary, the everyday, the routine, and chooses to bless them, to make them divine.

So if the first option wasn't true, then the second must be: these spiritual disciplines were possible for me as a parent of young kids if I simply tried harder. Right? But there seemed to be a trap there as well.

Often our churches—mine included—emphasize *trying harder. Doing more. Being better.* This focus strips the gospel of its central truth: Jesus came down to rescue us because *we could not save ourselves.* If the spiritual disciplines modeled and taught in Scripture are given by God for our good and his glory, then they simply could not be about just trying harder, or they'd be the opposite of the good gifts God wants to give us through them. God is about grace, not works. Love, not exhausted striving. Our obedience, properly ordered, flows from a connection with the God of life; it's not something we do for him as a way to earn his favor. As Hudson Taylor once put it, "God's work done in God's way never lacks God's supplies."[1]

Plus, parenthood itself has enough exhausted striving. Who among us hasn't been so tired our eyelashes hurt? Who hasn't been woken up at an ungodly hour by a toddler speaking the most dreaded four words: "I just threw up…"? Who among us hasn't done more heavy lifting in a single day of parenting than in four years of high school gym class? Even if I wanted to, I simply *couldn't* muscle more hours or willpower into my day. Sure, there were hours I could use better than I commonly did (social media addiction, anyone?), but there were also many days when surviving until that magical hour when both kids were finally asleep felt Herculean. If someone told me God was disappointed that I didn't also fast, pray, and read sixteen chapters of Scripture that day, I'd wonder if that God really loved me at all.

But perhaps there is a *third way*. And maybe that third way has something to do with grace—that spiritual practices are possible for anyone at any time, even parents, because the God who created us and loves us wants us to draw near and has provided tools to help us do so. Perhaps that same God is already at work within us, sanctifying us through the constant daily grind of loving littles. Perhaps the God who created my family and yours gave us these children to *help* us on the road to holiness, not to get in the way. It is entirely possible that because God wants us to be holy, he can and will make us so, even in this particularly exhausting season, if we will only let him.

I had no idea, really, if I could become a holy or even *almost* holy person while raising young kids. But I knew I needed to try. If we wait until we have the time, we will wait much too long. Perhaps even forever.

What I really longed for was a guide to spiritual disciplines for this intense season of parenthood, these difficult years in which I am responsible to keep tiny human beings alive and myself sane *at the same time*. When I began parenting, this guide simply didn't exist. Since then, Catherine McNiel published a lovely little book—*Long Days of Small Things*—that is well worth a read. Yet we need many more resources in this area, not fewer; so here I am, offering this little guide. Because Jesus loves me and my small people, and because he loves *you* and *your* small people, he wants to draw near to us here and now, not someday in the far off distance when we can find the time. Whether we're married or not, parents or not, men or women, young or old, Jesus cares deeply about the development of our souls. There are no exemptions to the call to follow Jesus.

So then, *how* do we cultivate spiritual disciplines—practices like prayer and fasting, meditation and contemplation, celebration, worship, and service—in the midst of one of life's more exhausting seasons? Is there a way that those spiritual disciplines can be practiced within the normal rhythms of parenthood so they are not just an addition to the never ending to-do list? Will these ancient disciplines even work outside a monastery or a pastor's study? Can a normal mom like me actually become holy?

I was determined to find out.

FOLDING THE HOLY INTO THE EVERYDAY

For an entire year, I would attach spiritual disciplines to routine parenting tasks in the hope of becoming a better disciple of Jesus and drawing closer to God, myself, my husband, and my kids. I'd write as I went, developing a guide for how to naturally fold the work of the spirit into the daily tasks of parenthood. Instead of adding more tasks to my already maxed-out days, I'd integrate spiritual practices into things I was already doing as a parent, from getting ready for the day in the morning to tucking my kids into bed at night.

Rather than map out my own journey in advance—which disciplines I'd take on during particular months—I decided to take a more organic approach. I'd begin with a simple practice and allow the leading of the Holy Spirit, the rhythm of the seasons, and the needs of our family to dictate which practice I took up next. This turned out to be quite an adventure, drawn out over a much longer time period than I originally anticipated. More on that later.

A bit about me as we begin. I'm a displaced midwesterner who reads too much and has never met a piece of candy I don't like. My husband Daryl and I have been married for eleven years, and we're parents to two boys. Our boys were seven weeks and three and a half years old, respectively, when I embarked on this project. As I write the final sentences, they're two and a half and six years old, and we are preparing to welcome a baby girl in just a few weeks. I'm also a co-pastor, serving alongside my husband at a Presbyterian church in southern California.

Stay with me here. Telling someone you're sitting next to on an airplane that you're a pastor is right up there with telling them you have irritable bowel syndrome. They look at me with pity or disgust or both and sometimes even try to find another seat. "Oh," their faces say, "you're one of those creepy holy people…"

Except, I'm *not* holy. I'm *so* not. I yell at my kids. I put off reading my Bible. I let swear words fly (sorry, Mom). But I *want* to be holy. Or at least holier than I am. Not in a holier-than-thou sort of way, but in the same way any follower of Jesus knows they must be if they are going to keep being a follower of Jesus at all. I'm on this journey, too. Being a pastor doesn't automatically make you holy any more than being a politician automatically makes you honest. Holiness must be sought.

As I've spoken to friends and congregants, at MOPS (mothers of preschoolers) gatherings and women's retreats, to parents young and old, near and far, I've discovered that this longing runs deep for many of us. We want—we *need*—more of Jesus. But amid the intense, unrelenting throes of parenthood, we aren't sure where to find him. The good news is we don't have to look far. As the psalmist writes, "Is anyone crying for help? God is listening, ready to rescue."[2] The ancient spiritual practices explored within the pages ahead can help open our eyes to this reality, connecting us more intimately to the Lord of life, teaching us to see him in the everyday moments, and preparing us to better hear his still, small voice.

This book is for us. It is for you.

CHAPTER 2

CAR RIDES & CONTEMPLATION
Finding Jesus on the Freeways

Formation remains a messy and imprecise business.
—James Wilhoit

The spiritual practice of contemplation felt like an obscure foreign country to me. I knew it existed, but I probably couldn't find it on a map. I certainly couldn't speak the language, and I'd definitely never *been* there.

The word conjured up images of brown-robed monks staring out upon swirling desert sands, and graying theologians poring over thick tomes in dusty libraries. To take time to contemplate anything—God, the world, nature—seemed like a luxury in a fast-paced world full of distractions and to-do lists. Back in college I'd steeped myself in contemplative poetry, but now my poetry books gathered dust.

"Seriously," I asked Daryl, "who has this much time to ponder a *flower*?"

Surely there were more profitable spiritual disciplines with which to begin this experiment. What about reading Scripture? What about *prayer*?

Yet the more I researched spiritual practices, the more contemplation seemed the place to start. It was simple—no books or props required. It would anchor me to Jesus—something I hungered for like a toddler who hasn't had a snack in hours. It was also novel—I'd never practiced contemplation before, at least not in any organized way.

CONTEMPLATION
THE SPIRITUAL DISCIPLINE OF PRACTICING THE AWARENESS OF THE PRESENCE OF JESUS.

PAUSING TO THINK DEEPLY ABOUT GOD AND MEDITATING ON HIS PRESENCE WITH, WITHIN, AND AROUND US.

As God-with-us, Jesus is always present in our midst. But how much time do we spend actually paying attention to him? I don't spend very much, to be honest. Less attention than I give to that ache in the middle of my lower back that is also always with me, but much less polite about it. If my yearlong experiment were to succeed, I would need lots of help from the Almighty. Tuning in to his presence looked like the area in which to begin.

There was one other reason I chose to begin with this particular discipline. Contemplation—stopping to sit with God, accept his love, soak it in—is a school for *being* rather than *doing*. In a season of life all about *doing*—the laundry, the preschool drop-off, the diaper, the dinner—*being* felt like exactly the lesson I needed.

It was, however, a lesson I didn't really have time for. What parent does? With a two-month-old baby sleeping only in random, few-hour chunks around the clock, I would immediately doze off if I sat still to contemplate the divine for more than a few seconds. (Sorry, Jesus.) All I was contemplating was my Starbucks order (venti *anything* caffeinated), whether or not I could squeeze in a shower before he woke back up (no), and how long it would be before I could fit into my pre-pregnancy jeans (an eternity and a half).

Yet because God is for everyone, the spiritual practices we find in the Scriptures truly are meant for us all, no matter the season of life in which we find ourselves. So I went back to the belief that began this whole ridiculous experiment: that because God wants us to draw near to him, spiritual disciplines can be adapted for anyone's current life situation, including mine. Including yours. Starting today. We cannot wait until our kids are grown to let God make us holier. So I pondered: How could I be a mom *and* a contemplative?

Describing the growth opportunities of this spiritual practice, Adele Ahlberg Calhoun writes, "Contemplatives are open to seeing the unseen world…they [are] alert to the transcendence in ordinary things."[3] That sounded delightful, since my current life was *overflowing* with ordinary. I still had a month of parental leave stretching out in front of me, and the long, full days included just me and my two littles with all the mundane ins and outs of young motherhood. I was hoping for survival; transcendence would be *great*.

Contemplation opens us to the understanding that the unremarkable is somehow sacred, too. That the same God who notices if a sparrow falls to the ground stays at my side as I explain to my preschooler for the eleven-thousandth time that just because he brushed his teeth yesterday doesn't mean he is off the hook today. The God who spoke creation into being is present to me as I soothe the baby to sleep, *again*, in the wee hours of the morning, kissing his downy head and waiting for the sun to rise. The God who came to earth to live and suffer and die and rise is nearer than my next breath as I sit on the couch in my maternity pants (no, I am not still pregnant…), staring despairingly and apathetically at the endless laundry mound in the corner of the living room, watching the moments tick away until Daryl comes home.

Chores and clothing and cuddles: these things are holy work. Parenting itself is holy work. God is with us and can be found in all that is around us—the tasks, the hours, the people. Reclaiming the common, everyday labor of bearing and raising and nurturing children as a divine practice, created and ordered and blessed by God, is a rich and wondrous calling. But my eyes were untrained. I often felt more drudgery than divinity. I complained far, *far* more than I contemplated.

So the first month's practice would be contemplation. A focus on *being with* God rather than *doing* things for him. Focusing on Jesus, being present to him, and remembering that he is with me and within me. In *A Celebration of Discipline,* Richard Foster describes it like this: "If we hope to move beyond the superficialities of our culture, including our religious culture, we must be willing to go down into the recreating silences, into the inner world of contemplation."[4] Likewise, the apostle Paul instructs us to "clothe yourselves with the Lord Jesus Christ,"[5] letting Jesus comfort and cover us like a perfectly fitted pair of jeans. In contemplation I would seek to respond to God's consistent presence with me in love, without *working* to earn his favor.

THE EXPERIMENT BEGINS

In a culture that moves as fast as ours and is filled with many distractions, easy visual reminders are key. Because my goal was to contemplate Jesus each and every day, I wanted to tie the spiritual practice to a natural and regular part of my routine. I decided to connect it to that most annoying and constant of parental tasks: driving. That's right—I was going to contemplate Jesus in the car.

Given that all I usually contemplated while in the car was how late we were running (does *everyone's* preschooler have to stop and examine every piece of bird poo between the house and the car?!), I needed some structure. Calhoun encourages believers to contemplate Jesus, others, and then their immediate experiences, turning an eye to God in the midst of the ordinary things of life.[6] That seemed a helpful tip. Rather than using my car rides as an opportunity to listen to episodes of *This American Life* with both kids immobilized in their car seats (even Ira Glass's melodious, soothing tenor can drown out the complaints of kids begging for more *Veggie Tales Christmas* if you turn him up loudly enough), I'd contemplate God. I'd follow Calhoun's advice to begin with Jesus and return to him when distractions arose.

That was it. I felt ready.

To my midwestern can-do, Protestant-work-ethic self, starting this experiment with a month of contemplation basically sounded like thirty days of doing nothing. I'd have nothing to show for my efforts at the month's end—not a cleaner house or a happier marriage or eighteen memorized chapters of Scripture—but with a seven-week-old baby and inexperience in most spiritual disciplines, it seemed wise to start small and simple.

I mean, really—how hard could it be?

DAY 1: THE LOGISTICS

The first drive of the experiment was to meet my friend Orva for a park playdate. Orva is the type of friend who texts, "What can I bring you from Peet's Coffee? Vanilla iced latte, right?" She offers to bring coffee *and* remembers my favorite. I freaking love Orva.

Since contemplation is designed to move us through a process, focusing first on the love of Jesus, then on others, and finally meditating on the world around us, I wrote a reminder on an envelope and taped it to my dashboard.

BREATHE

JESUS

OTHERS

OUTSIDE

I meant to print it out on pretty paper, but I ran out of time, so I scribbled it with a Sharpie on the back of half an envelope. Just keeping it real. Wilson had been up half the night (seriously, the kid is an *eater!*), so I knew I'd forget to contemplate much of anything without a visual to grab my attention.

Because contemplation isn't meant to be done in a hurry, *Breathe* was a reminder to me to take a few deep breaths before starting. Easy peasy.

I buckled the kiddos into their seats, Wilson already dozing. I gave Linc a baggie of almonds, because snacks are the only secret I knew to securing a few moments of peace and quiet with a precocious preschooler, and I paused to take three deep breaths in the driver's seat before hitting the road. It felt like a long time to make the kids wait. To make *me* wait.

Lord, I give you this month. This year. This drive.

By the time we turned out of our street I saw a lady wearing a cute tank top and wondered where she got it and whether *I* should get one and if it'd help hide my postpartum tummy and already I'd forgotten about Jesus and it had been literally thirty seconds. So I went back to him again. *Jesus, Jesus, Jesus. Is that really all I'm supposed to do while I'm in the car? For a month?* I began to imagine what it would be like if Jesus was in the car with me.

Wait—Jesus is in the car. He's always with me. He promises that. So …why do I forget so very often? Jesus, you're here.

Within seconds I was flooded with gratitude and wonder. Jesus was in my car. I glanced back at my two kids, one sleeping and one munching, and felt this overwhelming, heart-grabbing, gut-punching love for them. Then it hit me. *That same love I have for my kids? Jesus loves them that much. Jesus loves me that much. MORE, even.* My eyes filled up with tears. I pulled down my sunglasses. Ten minutes in and I was already crying.

It was going to be a long month.

DAY 3: FINDING JESUS IN EVERY DAY

The practice of contemplation is, at its heart, the practice of awakening to the work of God in us and in the world. Annie Dillard once wrote that "beauty and grace are performed whether or not we will or sense them. The least we can do is try to be there."[7] God is at work, and I wanted to tune in to that work. To show up, eyes opened. But it turns out that being present to God's work is…well, it's *hard work.*

Today's drive was to a local government office. Our newest addition, Wilson, was born in a hippie birth center because we are *those* people, so I had to go to the Social Security office to get him registered in the system. I buckled him in, and as we drove, I contemplated some holy mysteries.

I wonder what you think about Social Security, Jesus, I mused. *Ha! I've never thought about that before. I wonder if that's part of what contemplation is supposed to do—to help me realize that God is in all of life, not just the "spiritual parts."*

In his Romans doxology, the apostle Paul praises God because "from him and through him and to him are all things."[8] Not some things or many things, but *everything.* Even our local Social Security office, with its long lines and mounds of paperwork, a place where I wouldn't necessarily go looking for Jesus.

DAY 5: IN WHICH I REALIZE I LACK THE PATIENCE FOR THIS

Wilson wailed. He was hungry, but I didn't want to feed him in the scalding Target parking lot—southern California in June feels like the surface of the sun—so I was trying to get us home quickly, and (of course) we hit every single red light. *Jesus, Jesus, Jesus.*

Linc started yelling then, too. I didn't take my deep breaths. I was so tired that just keeping my eyes open felt like lifting weights. This experiment was too hard for me. Being a Christian was too hard for me. I contemplated joining some sort of a cult with sister-wives so I could have daytime help.

I decided to postpone practicing the discipline of contemplation until fifty years in the future, when I'd be in a nursing home. Maybe I would have time for it then.

DAY 7: CONTEMPLATION WITH OTHERS

Friday is our family day off, our Sabbath (the church expects pastors to work SUNDAYS! The nerve!), so we headed to the beach. We meant to leave by 8 a.m., but since one of our cars got towed from the street in front of our condo the night before (oh, Orange County and your insane parking regulations…), we spent the morning—and $280 we didn't have—getting it back from the impound. Needless to say, tensions were running high.

By 10:30 a.m.(!) we were finally in the car, along with a diaper bag, cooler full of water and snacks, bag of towels, giant sunshade, bucket of sand toys, two strollers, two kids, and Daryl and me, both borderline radioactive with crankiness. One of the boys was crying, and the other was fake crying because "Wilson's crying is making me scared."

I took my three deep breaths and tried to contemplate Jesus. That he was present with us and in us. That, in his infinite mercy, he just might keep us from the brink of a serious marital meltdown where we both say things we shouldn't. Exhaustion and crying children tend to loosen the tongue.

"I'm hungry." Linc stopped fake crying and was now ready for a snack. And why not, he had only had two breakfasts. I passed back carrots and hummus.

"I want a song." I turned on a folk CD.

"How do you want me to treat this experiment?" asked my husband. "Can I talk to you?"

What I wanted to say was, "Please don't, we are both grouchy beyond repair, and the car might explode." But I didn't. I said, "Part of contemplation is being present to and aware of the people around you, so go ahead." He paused. I paused. *Jesus*, I sighed. *Jesus, Jesus, Jesus.*

I glanced over and noticed the bags under his eyes. I wasn't the only one losing sleep with a newborn in the house. On top of serving as a pastor, he was working early mornings and late nights and almost every Saturday to finish his dissertation and graduate with his PhD. He'd injured a knee weeks earlier and was days away from surgery, spending every moment he was on his feet in sharp, grabbing pain. For the first time in weeks, I truly saw him. I reached over and squeezed his hand.

"How are *you*?" I asked, not because I'd achieved maximum holiness but because Jesus gives grace and helps us to see. Daryl sighed.

"I'm tired."

"Me too."

We filled up the car with gas and then drove the toll road—a special treat, since it costs over seven dollars each way and that is absolute nonsense. But the main road wouldn't get us to the beach until naptime, and that'd just be depressing. The hills rolled by. I passed the preschooler more snacks.

I don't know if I was just too tired to contemplate Jesus, but I ended up with a blank mind, watching the desert hills go by. Jesus was there somewhere.

As I looked for him, I remembered—he was with us in the car. He created the hills we were passing, the ocean we were headed toward. Inside each of the ceramic-tile-roofed homes down in the valley below, he was present. For a minute, in the tiny quiet space in my mind between talking to Daryl and listening to Lincoln belt out the lyrics to "Tingalayo" (*My donkey dance, my donkey sing, my donkey wearing a diamond ring!* OMG. WHY.), it blew my mind.

Then the spell was broken as I was summoned for more snacks.

DAY 9: ON FAILING SPECTACULARLY

Daryl and I met at Wheaton College, a school dedicated "to Christ and his kingdom," filled with former homeschoolers, child prodigies, and other spiritual overachievers. I grew up in the Evangelical Free Church, so it was at Wheaton that I first discovered liturgical traditions with their smells and bells and church calendars. In a nearby Anglican church, I first learned that there were dozens more Christian holidays than just Easter and Christmas—there was Pentecost, Ascension, Epiphany. Trinity Sunday preceded World Communion Sunday. Easter came only after Palm Sunday, Maundy Thursday, and Good Friday. For the first time, keeping track of my spiritual life wasn't just between me and Jesus and a pastor or two. I'd stumbled into a faith tradition vastly deeper than I'd ever imagined. There were paraments and vestments, connections to the global church, appreciation for historic Christianity, and figures like St. Augustine, Thomas Aquinas, and Catherine of Siena. They professed an openness to healing prayer. I was awed and a little bit freaked out, but since so many upperclassmen I respected attended the church, I decided to give it a try.

It was in their company during my sophomore year of college that I dove into the spiritual practices of Lent for the first time. A hyperactive conscience is a tough thing to overcome, though, and in an eager misinterpretation of an ancient Christian practice, I quickly turned it into a new form of trying to be good enough for God. If I gave up sugar for forty days, surely he would be impressed and love me more, right?

One morning in my Christian formation class, Dr. Tim Larsen, thoughtful historian and scholar, gazed out over his students with a grin.

"You all doing well at your Lenten practices?" he asked. We nodded, proudly. We were *super* holy. "You do know that part of what Lent is supposed to teach us is that we are weak and can't earn our salvation, right?" he asked. "If you don't fail at least once, you aren't doing Lent right." I balked at his words then—who was he to tell me I couldn't muscle my way to holy living?—but they've been balm for my soul in this season of contemplation.

Take today, for example. We were headed to a friend's house, and I promised I'd bring muffins, which was stupid because I knew we'd be running late, and sure enough, we were loading up at the exact time I told her we'd be arriving. I hate being late. I'm too German to be late to things. That and my chronically early dad once told me that when a person is late, whoever is waiting spends their time thinking about the late person's flaws. Yeah, that didn't make me neurotic *at all*.

So we were already late, and preschoolers can sense when you're running late, and it turns them into banana slugs.

"Can you get in the car, Linc?" I asked him, juggling Wilson's twelve-pound bucket car seat with fourteen-pound Wilson in it, plus the diaper bag and the basket of muffins, wondering how on earth I hadn't lost all the baby weight yet since I was always carrying so much crap everywhere.

"Yessssss…" He meandered to his car door and looked up at his car seat like it was Mount Kilimanjaro.

"Lincoln, NOW."

"Oh-KAAAAY." Was three and a half years old a little soon to be such an eye-roller? I buckled him in, snapped Wilson's car seat into its latches, and we were on our way. It was three miles down the road (out of a five-mile drive) before I realized I forgot to breathe *or* pray. And I had a reminder taped to the blessed dashboard.

At least Dr. Larsen gets me.

DAY 11: DIGITAL DISTRACTIONS

Is it terrible that the hardest part of practicing contemplation has been not using my cell phone in the car? I know, I know, shame on me for ever using it at all while behind the wheel. I don't use it while the car is in motion, but I text at stoplights or fiddle with music on the regular. It's a problem; technology is often an enemy of discipleship. It numbs us and fries us and separates us from God, ourselves, our neighbors, and the world around us. I'm willing to bet most monasteries don't allow smartphones.

When I started this experiment, I planned to keep my phone in the glove compartment, but I forgot one crucial thing: I get lost. A lot. I'm the kind of person who did okay living in Chicago because it's built on a grid and one fourth of that grid is Lake Michigan, so there are only three directions to worry about. I still got lost, but less often. Southern California road maps look like a bowl of Ramen. Nothing goes in a straight line, mountains and canyons litter the landscape, and dozens of roads in South County make nearly a circle so you can't just find the right road and feel out which way to turn. I use my GPS constantly. Because I can't hear my phone directing me from the glove compartment, it stays in the center console, but I've prohibited myself from using it for anything but directions this month. It's pretty darned near impossible to contemplate Jesus with texts coming in.

But today? Today I picked it up four times in the ten minutes it took us to get to our babysitter's graduation party. We love her so much we kind of hoped she would fail out of school so that she could babysit Lincoln forever, but I guess that was sort of selfish and anyway she went ahead and graduated with honors. We are bringing a journal and a Target gift card and two little boys, one of whom was super excited to be invited to a high schooler's party, and the other of whom was super excited because he suspected he would get to nurse at some point.

The phone sat in the center console between Daryl and me. He was driving, and normally I'd be on that phone, because I don't get much time to tech it up when I'm watching the kids. I never looked at it, but the habit was so deeply ingrained in me that I kept grabbing for it. Then I felt bored. Then guilty. Then I'd think about Jesus. *Jesus, Jesus, Jesus. I'm bored. I'm tired, too. I wonder if anyone has texted me…*

I can't tell if I'm bad at contemplating Jesus and always will be, or if I just need to be patient in order for more to be revealed. I hope it's the former. Patience is *so* not my thing.

DAY 14: CONTEMPLATING FORGIVENESS

Half of our small group called in sick tonight, which isn't unusual. Between the four couples, we have five kids ages three and under, and eight kids total, so there is nearly always someone down with the stomach flu or a nasty cold. Last year we studied Ephesians, but I had a baby a couple of months ago, and between that and flu season frequently halving our group, it's been too overwhelming to study anything substantive. So for these weeks we let the littles play while the adults fix dinner. I nurse the baby, and we all share prayer requests and talk about the deep things and the small things that make up life.

Tonight on the drive over, Daryl was in a state because Lincoln didn't nap that afternoon despite both of our best efforts, so he turned into a tiny Tyrannosaurus. (Lincoln, not Daryl, though Daryl was on his way there too, now that I mention it.) Because I struggle with not feeling what everyone else in the room is feeling, I quickly grew grouchy, too. Wilson was the only one in the car not in a funk.

We talked about discipline tactics and what to do with Lincoln when he's out-of-control hyper, as he was that day. It can be hard to tell with a three-year-old what is purposeful naughtiness and what is just overtiredness or developmentally appropriate boundary-testing.

Linc quickly melted down once we arrived, dumping buckets of toys onto the floor and refusing to help clean them up, kicking and screaming in a Tasmanian-devil-worthy tantrum, probably the worst he'd ever had, and we left early and embarrassed, despite our friends' assurances that every kid has moments like this.

On the way home I didn't contemplate anything but how to get back on the same page with Daryl, how to train our son not to be a human pinball machine when he grows up, and how very tired we all were. Daryl and I spoke harshly to Lincoln, and then to each other, and then slowly, ever-so-slowly, began to warm and apologize as the miles turned beneath our wheels. Which was, in a way, a sort of prayer.

I have to believe that when families look each other in the eye and say, "I'm sorry, we could have done that better," Jesus is so deeply glorified. The mess of family is a place where the Holy Spirit is alive and moving, even when evenings end in tantrums instead of tidy goodbyes.

DAY 16: FAILING SOME MORE

I was failing at contemplation. Like *seriously* failing. Spectacularly, absolutely, completely failing. I got in the car today and thought about Jesus not at all, despite my visual reminders. I texted at stoplights because I just couldn't help it. (Well, I could have helped it, but I didn't.) Some days in newbornlandia leave me feeling like a hollow shell of a person, completely tapped out by the kids and their constant, incessant needs. To nurse. To sleep. To have breakfast—no, not *this* toast, the *other* kind of toast. To hear a story when I'm so tired my eyes won't focus. To have their messes cleaned up. To be wiped on the potty. To nurse. To nurse. To nurse. To nurse.

I needed a friend, so I spent my stoplight time texting my girlfriend Becky instead of contemplating Jesus because, quite frankly, I knew Becky would understand and I wasn't sure Jesus would. The guy *had* no kids, and as ill-behaved as his disciples were from time to time, I bet none of them pooped on the floor right before company came over. I get that he "knows our weakness," but he doesn't text back. So I reached out for a friend, who responded back immediately with words of grace and kindness, and I felt instant relief—she gets it!—and then utter shame—I've failed at this contemplation exercise again! And I'm a *pastor*!

Then God brought Paul's words from Romans 5 to my mind, in an act of divine mercy. Jesus came *while we were still sinners.* If he loved me then, perhaps he loves me now. And here's a really radical thought—maybe failure is actually part of the point of contemplating the presence of Jesus. Spiritual disciplines give us time and space to really feel the depth of our frailty, our separation from God, our animalistic wants and desires, and how easily and quickly we ignore the good.

It hurts. But in understanding and maybe even accepting that I am far from the master of my own soul—I can't even go a couple of days without texting in the car—I'm beginning to believe and love God more, as I learn to trust that his love depends only on him, not on my performance.

I'm a mess, and he still thinks I'm great. So I guess I'll try again tomorrow. I suppose I can give him at least one more day to make something out of me. Good luck, Jesus.

DAY 17: THE LONG, HARD LESSON OF GRACE

Something about owning up to yesterday's failure helped to free me today. I'm not *going* to be good at this. Trying to contemplate Jesus in the midst of motherhood is not a skill I was born with, and contemplating Jesus *at all* is not something I've ever done. So I'm *going* to fail. Impressively. But then maybe I can try again. It was Watchman Nee who once advised, "When you are reduced to utter weakness and are persuaded that you can do nothing whatsoever, then God will do everything."[9] Praise him for that.

Do you know what? Today *was* better. God is patient. Day by day I am beginning to remember to go back to Jesus. I'm beginning to expect that he will be with me in errand-running and appointment-keeping. It's almost as if success isn't the point—*returning* is. The structure, the rhythm, the grace of these disciplines is that they remain even when we are inconstant and unsteady. A person who has never practiced contemplation can start today for the first time, and the Holy Spirit will begin a good work within her. My faltering steps in this practice were still steps. Even if we only take one or two or three in a month, God uses each of those steps. The goal isn't perfection. The goal is that you and I go back to Jesus again and again and all over again.

Today I drove the boys to a playdate at a trampoline park. I was distracted by a thousand things, but I watched each of the distractions come and then let them go and turned back to Jesus. I'm learning.

It's odd, though: practicing a discipline but having nothing tangible to show for it. I used to be a runner, and I loved that after a few weeks I would start to feel a difference in my endurance, my stamina, how my pants fit. But contemplation? If I do it well, I'll have a quieter spirit and a more responsive soul, which is not a thing I can show off like a perfectly trimmed rosebush or a fantastically frosted cake.

It just *is*. I mean, it isn't *yet*, but hopefully it will be.

DAY 20: CONTEMPLATING WITHOUT THE CAR

My friend Kristy, a widowed mom of three ginormous boys, once told me, "Some days I just set the bar right on the ground. That way I know I am getting over it." Amen, sister.

Daryl had knee surgery a couple of days ago, so he wasn't allowed to drive yet. Plus, he needed constant supervision until he weaned off the painkillers, meaning I was stuck at home, too. He continued to mend well but remained in that post-surgery funk that turns people into dwarves. (You know, Grumpy, Sleepy, Dopey, and all the rest?) I was exhausted from caring for not just an infant and a preschooler but a thirty-something, too. Everyone needed a snack. Everyone needed a blanket. Everyone needed to be reassured that mommy's here, mommy loves them. Everyone needed, needed, *needed*.

At one point Daryl chastised me for working so hard, and I contemplated smothering him with a pillow because *what am I supposed to do? Not feed the baby? Let my stitched-up husband crawl over to the freezer to refill his giant ice cooler himself?* Instead I ate half a can of chocolate frosting and plotted retreating to a distant island as soon as the baby was weaned.

Part of the rub of spiritual disciplines is that it's both easier and harder to practice them when life is running smoothly. On a normal day, a day when I've had some sleep and some food and some fresh air, I often forget to turn to Jesus because I feel self-sufficient. But on a difficult day, one where sleep is elusive and there isn't enough time to do all that needs to be done, I viscerally understand my need for Jesus, yet the spiritual feelings of peace and contentment are nowhere to be found. It turns out we need both hills and valleys to fully develop as followers of Jesus. So I'm trying to find my way back to him, time and again, in the midst of the chaos of life.

Theologian N. T. Wright notes that love is much less an ephemeral feeling and much more a practiced act. "[Love] is a language to be learned, a musical instrument to be practiced, a mountain to be climbed via some steep and tricky cliff paths but with the most amazing view from the top."[10] I hoped to get some of that view, soon, because the air was pretty thick with fog down here.

DAY 22: STEEP AND TRICKY INDEED

The baby woke to eat four times last night, and wet through his diaper once, necessitating an outfit-and-swaddle-sack change and an entire soothe-to-sleep routine. Not a small thing, since it currently takes him two hours to fall back to sleep. A couple of weeks ago I bragged on Facebook that my baby was sleeping through the night, because I'm a dolt. *Why* did I tempt fate? I want to give my past self a smack upside the head.

Daryl weaned himself off his pain meds and felt well enough to be on his own today, so Wilson and I drove to the pediatrician for a ten-week checkup. He wailed in the backseat because he was overtired, because he was too grumpy to take a morning nap, because he was already overtired. It was a vicious cycle, and I couldn't stop it. There's something about an infant's cry that frazzles my nerves like nothing else. My milk lets down even if he just ate, and my brain starts to pulse with a constant *RED ALERT! BABY IS SAD!* making it nearly impossible for me to think straight. I briefly wondered if I was safe to drive.

As he continued to wail, I started speaking to him like I would an IRS auditor. "Hey there, sir, can you cut me a *break*?"

It was days like these, so back-breakingly exhausting I could barely pour my own coffee, let alone behave civilly toward a screaming child, that I hated this spiritual disciplines experiment. Like *really* hated it. I felt guilty the moment I got into my car because, quite frankly, I didn't *want* to talk to God or meditate on him. I was barely surviving; I didn't have time for spiritual crap.

It was in the middle of one of these rants (in my head only, since the baby had finally dozed off in his car seat) that God broke through to me.

I'm here to help.

Wait, what?

I love you.

Uh, yeah. I'm super unlovable right now, but thanks anyway.

Contemplation is an exercise in grace.

Grace…Hm. I'm better at guilt than grace.

I'd love to teach you.

In the moments of car travel when I actually remembered I was supposed to be contemplating God, I often tried to pray the Jesus prayer. It's a simple prayer, designed to be timed to a person's breathing (which also reminds me to *breathe*, which is never a bad thing).

Breathe in. *Lord, Jesus Christ.*

Breathe out. *Son of God.*

Breathe in. *Have mercy on me.*

Breathe out. *A sinner.*

In my lowest moments, praying this prayer has felt like self-flagellation. I *know* I'm a sinner. I yelled at my kid getting into the car. I ignored my husband last night when he wanted to talk. I often care more about my pants size than any of the starving people in the world. I'm a dirty sinner. *I get it.*

But the more I prayed this prayer, the more God began to open my eyes to what it really means to be a sinner. I've sinned, of course. I've done bad things and failed to do good ones, even today. Even this hour. But part of being a sinner means that my eyes aren't fully opened to the spiritual realities all around me. My senses are dulled to what God wants to say and do in and through me. Being a sinner is like trying to run a marathon on two broken legs. Even though I may have broken them myself, they still hurt. Being a sinner means being lost and exhausted and scared and sad. This is why Jesus came.

This prayer began to turn to grace in my mind as I said it, not knowing anything else to say. *Have mercy on me. Lord Jesus Christ. Have mercy on me, a sinner.*

DAY 25: ADVENTURE PARK

Daryl went back to work yesterday, but today was his day off, so we celebrated by immediately having a fight. Do you ever notice that this seems to happen more when you and those you love have open-ended time together? Right before a vacation, maybe, or at the start of a long weekend?

So we were fighting, because the morning got away from us both. We each pulled time from the other in little selfish ways: he took a ridiculously long shower; I wasted time on my computer instead of being quick to get dressed. The kids suffered, the hour suffered, and then all of a sudden it was 95 degrees outside, well past time for the baby's morning nap, and we were loading the car and silently loathing each other for causing the problem we both caused. Ah, marital bliss.

As we drove to the park, I sat silently and stared at the note on the passenger side's dash. *Breathe. Jesus. Others. Outside.*

Ok, Jesus, what would you have me do with my impossible husband? Because he is IMPOSSIBLE.

I pulled down my sunglasses, stared out the window, and hoped that the tiff would pass. Dissipate somehow into the roasting hot morning air. But it didn't, so we had to *talk* about it. We hashed it out and I cried and he ruminated and the kiddos were silent in the backseat. Wilson slept, but Lincoln was wide-eyed, alternately watching the cars pass by out the window and watching Mommy and Daddy work out the kinks of the morning.

We didn't yell, but the tone was tense. *Jesus, come. Speak peace.* Every few minutes we reassured Linc that Mommy and Daddy love each other but sometimes disagree and have to figure things out. He nodded.

It's no surprise to me that loving God and one another are Scripture's two greatest commandments. There is no greater call, no greater good, and no greater challenge. Within families where we live closely and rely heavily on one another, this call is particularly difficult. According to N. T. Wright, "Christianity is a personal relationship of love and loyalty to the one who has loved us more than we can begin to imagine. And the test of that love and loyalty remains the simple, profound, dangerous, and difficult command: love one another."[11] Nowhere did the command to love one another feel more profound today than in caring for this marriage.

By the time we arrived at the park, my eyes were red and puffy, but shalom had been restored. Daryl was wrong. I was wrong. We were working it out. We did work it out. And somewhere Jesus was smiling.

DAY 26: PRAYING FOR PARKING SPACES

It was over 90 degrees out again today, and the kids and I were headed to a splash pad for a playdate with Lincoln's preschool class. The school year ended Tuesday, and already everyone missed each other. Linc recited the names of all his friends as we drove the few miles. *Bradley. Matthew. Parker. Annie. Will Annie be there, Mommy? Audrey. Charley. Charlotte. Jackson.* Our shy little three-year-old blossomed into a talkative and confident little guy in school this year, and I was grateful.

The drive wasn't long enough to do much contemplating, but I *did* practice an art most parents of youngsters are well equipped in: praying for a parking space. There is questionable theology here.

On the one hand: Praying for a *parking space*, really? Is my car more important than everyone else's? Of all the things I could speak to God about, is convenience what I want to bring to him? With all the wars and rumors of wars out there, should I bother God with such nonsense?

On the other hand: If God cares for every sparrow, surely the worry I feel in having to lug two kids, a swim bag, and a heavy cooler up two sets of stairs is something he cares about too, right? I didn't know. I was too tired to decide if it was theologically okay to pray about it. So I just prayed about it.

I checked the little alcove closest to the splash pad. It has two parking spots, and they are never, ever open.

Except today.

Thank you, Jesus.

DAY 27: A DRIVE ALONE

This was the first drive I took in this whole experiment without at least one of the kids in the car. I was headed to a coffee shop near the ocean to read and write and regain some of the bits of selfhood that were lost during the first few weeks of acting as a feeding trough for a newborn. Daryl took the kids to the park to give me two blissful hours on my own. He'd offered me more time, but I didn't want to lug a breast pump on my tour of freedom.

The road wound up and over the coastal hills until I crested the final one, only to be gobsmacked by a dazzling ocean view. The Pacific. White-sailed boats and whale spouts and the whole nine.

You're welcome, I felt Jesus say. *I love you.*

DAY 28: A SNAIL'S PACE, BUT PROGRESS NONETHELESS

I recapped how this month has gone with Daryl and my friend Anna last night, telling them it felt kind of like a failure, and Daryl broke in: "Are you kidding me? You're way different with the kids than you were a month ago. Much less overwhelmed. I haven't seen you with them in the car much, but at home you seem more present and less stressed. Maybe you feel like it didn't work, but it sure looks to me like it did."

I once heard someone describe reading Scripture like pouring water into a basket. It might seem like it all just flowed out through the cracks, like nothing really stuck. But after pouring water into the basket for a while, that basket is *soaked*. It is changed.

Maybe that's the best way to look at this past month's spiritual discipline. The basket of my life isn't holding anything different, but it's nice and soggy. Surely that's the start of becoming just a little bit more holy.

DAY 30: LESSONS FROM THE JOURNEY

I'll admit that I assumed I'd be farther along by the end of this month. My own consumerist attitude surprises me, though perhaps it shouldn't. Commercialism is the stew we all swim in. *I contemplated Jesus for a few minutes a day for a whole month! Where are my results!?* Still, despite my lack of patience with the process, God is faithful, and the past thirty days have indeed taught me a couple of things:

1) **The work of God is slow.** I hate this. I like to go *fast*. I like to get things *done*. I can write a blog post in ten minutes (not a *good* one, but still!), clean the kitchen in

fifteen, and organize the whole playroom before you can say, "Why'd you let the toys pile up for so long?" Yet the work of God is slow. Often just achingly, achingly slow. Like most good things, holiness will take time.

2) **Jesus is here.** Here in the car. Here in my home. Here between me and my kids and my husband. When I call on him, he answers. When I cry out to him, he brings peace. He is so very, very good. I wish I'd begun to notice him sooner.

Still, the journey is far from over. I'm excited now. If a single month of contemplation could begin to wake me up to the work of God in the world like this, what might the next ones hold?

JOIN THE JOURNEY

Contemplation is a delightfully simple spiritual practice. Think about Jesus—who he is, what he's done for you, how much he loves you. When your thoughts wander, let them go without worry or shame and come back to Jesus. If you plan to practice it in the car, as I did, it may help you to put the same visual reminder on your dashboard:

Breathe
Jesus
Others
Outside

The following passages of Scripture may help to aid you in your contemplation:

Psalm 23
Psalm 121
Isaiah 55:1–5
Matthew 11:28–30
Romans 11:33–36

CHAPTER 3

SLEEPYTIME & SERVICE
Sacrificial Love at the End of a Long Day

*Bedtime makes you realize how completely incapable
you are of being in charge of another human being.*
—Jim Gaffigan

When I look at an average day in my parenting life, one hour stands out as the time it's hardest to be patient, kind, and loving. Not the early mornings; God made coffee for that. Not midday, though on the days my kids don't nap I run low on patience. No, by far the hardest, most difficult, most soul-crushing time of day is the hour before the kids go to bed.

I mean, think about it. The kids wake up early, like am-I-being-punished-for-something-early, in the morning, needing snacks and wanting to pour eight bajillion Legos onto the living room floor before I've even formed a coherent sentence. My infant's nursing off and on all night, so I haven't even had the chance to miss him. The preschooler balks at getting dressed, and I've given up repeating the lecture that putting clothes on is just something people *do* and no we can't go to Costco without pants. I wrestle him into a shirt, cajole him into using the potty, throw a half-dozen snacks into my purse, find my missing wallet (already in my purse), keys (blessedly on their hook in the kitchen for once), and phone (somehow wedged between the cushions of the only couch I never sit on), and get us out the door. Then this type of thing continues for the next *twelve to fourteen hours*. Know what I mean? By bedtime, "tapped out" isn't the half of where most parents are. Exhausted doesn't begin to describe it. Try typhoid tired.

So by the time baths and books and songs and last-minute cuddles arrive, I don't *want* to snuggle and soothe my babies. I want someone *else* to do that while I sit alone, pop open a grape soda, turn on endless reruns of *The Office*, and eat popcorn until I die. But I'm not allowed to do that because I have been entrusted with precious humans who can't yet put themselves to bed, and deep inside I know that outsourcing bedtime seven nights a week (even imagining we could remotely afford such a thing) would make me sad someday when my kids are grown. Not today, but you know, *someday*.

I've backpacked through Scotland, climbed to the top of nameless canyons, and led whitewater kayaking excursions for kids in the Wisconsin wilderness. I'm not a whiner or a pushover, but man, bedtime is haaaaaaard. It just really is. Doing it once is difficult. Doing it every night until they go the heck to sleep on their own is like swimming the English Channel wearing ankle weights.

To make matters even more difficult, our newborn isn't in any kind of routine yet. He's only a few months old, so he's still not sure when it's day and when it's not, but for whatever reason, he tends to cry from 7 p.m. until 9 p.m., like clockwork, every single blessed night. We've tried everything—swaddling, unswaddling, nursing, fresh diapers, a pacifier, a walk in the stroller, setting his crib on an incline, begging and pleading and singing the theme song from *Friends* while standing on one foot by an open window (hey, it worked for a couple of minutes...), but no dice. The pediatrician says he'll grow out of it and that it's just a touch of colic, but it turns our evenings into quite dispiriting events.

Daryl often attends late-night meetings, so by the time he walks in the door, Wilson has usually been squalling his little head off for hours. As soon as I hear the lock click open, I dump the swaddled baby in Daryl's arms like a squirmy, spit-up-flavored taquito and go for a walk around the block because I just *cannot* anymore.

SERVICE
ASSISTING AND CARING FOR OTHERS WITH THE
LOVE, KINDNESS, AND COMPASSION OF JESUS.

Even if you're past the phase involving a newborn, the average bedtime routine with kids provides constant opportunity for disaster. They are tired; you are tired. They *know* you're tired, so often the temptation to be naughty, to dawdle, to push *all the buttons* is just too much for them to resist. They also have remarkably bad spatial awareness late at night. My three-year-old sometimes steps out of the bathtub and immediately goes totally limp just for fun, resulting in him crashing to the tile floor in a heap of tears.

Him: That huuuuuurt!

Me: What did you *think* was going to happen?

Whoever coined the phrase "God never gives you more than you can handle" never had kids. (Or read the Bible, because that sentiment isn't in there *anywhere*. But I digress.)

Don't get me wrong, I *love* my kids. I'm crazy about them. They're amazing and fascinating little people and I would fight a bear for them. And even when they've pushed all my buttons, the deepest prayer of my heart remains that they would grow up to know the radical, unabashed, incomprehensible love of the Jesus who adores them, even when they've gone limp outside the bathtub for no earthly reason. Especially then.

Yet if I don't know the love of Jesus for *me*, I certainly can't pass it on to them. So after last month's contemplation experiment, I was hungry this month for God's help in turning me outward toward my kids. I wanted to find ways to be more present to them, even when I'm exhausted. I needed to learn to dance the two-kid tango with grace instead of barely surviving. Still, I wasn't sure what discipline God wanted me to dive into this month until I read Richard Foster's thoughts on service. "As the cross is the sign of submission," he wrote, "so the towel is the sign of service."[12] Since many of our evenings end with baths, it seemed perfect. I wanted to use the bedtime hour as a chance to serve my kids—and thus, Jesus—rather than simply trying to clean them, pajama them, and shovel them into bed so I could collapse in a heap.

This would undoubtedly be *quite* a challenge. Small, repeated acts of service can be the most difficult of all. Early on in marriage, Daryl and I pledged, starry-eyed, that we would die for each other, but when the realities of living together began to set in, the everyday annoyances and duties and disagreements and squabbles quickly helped us realize that neither one of us was willing to sacrifice certain small things. I'd gladly donate a kidney to him if he needed one, but I wasn't going to let him wipe his toothpaste-encrusted face on our guest towels. He'd give his life to push me out of the way of a speeding bus, but he wasn't about to let me pick out a living room lamp, because apparently I don't "understand design aesthetic," whatever that means.

Turns out it's sometimes easier to bend and love and serve in the big things. Foster describes it this way: "Radical self-denial gives the feel of adventure. If we forsake all, we even have the chance of glorious martyrdom. But in service we must experience the many little deaths of going beyond ourselves. Service banishes us to the mundane, the ordinary, the trivial."[13] There's absolutely nothing glamorous about service. Millions of people know of Mother Teresa, but only a handful know a single name of any of the hundreds of other nuns and thousands of volunteers who worked with her over the years in Calcutta. To serve is to be behind the scenes, willingly giving heart and hands without any expectation of acknowledgment or recompense. To serve is, by and large, to fade into the background. In parenthood, as in discipleship, it is to die to ourselves daily: exactly what Jesus invites us to do.

After all, it is the mundane, ordinary, trivial parts of parenthood that can be the most brutal. Anyone can fold a basket of laundry with good cheer, but a hundred and forty baskets each year for twenty years? I'm pretty sure even Mother Teresa would have had a *few* grumpy moments when faced with that Sisyphean task. Yet life is made up of these tiny, trivial acts of service that, when taken together, are nowhere near tiny or trivial. They can communicate love or carelessness, kindness or cruelty, humility or pride. Learning to serve our kids with the humility and love of Christ is a lesson that will bear fruit in every other area of our lives, and theirs.

REQUIRED ACTS, FREELY GIVEN KINDNESSES

But hang on, you may be asking. Don't parents *have* to serve their kids? How is this a spiritual discipline? You have a point. On one hand, as a mom I have no choice but to attend to my kids. They have to be fed, clothed, slept, and carted to and fro, or someone will take them away from me (and with good reason!). But I can perform all these tasks without ever truly *serving* them. I can undertake these duties with a victim complex, begrudgingly or angrily; I can even accomplish them with disdain. I can shop and cook and feed and clothe, all while bewailing how difficult my kids, my husband, and my life are.

It isn't that parents—even Christian ones—aren't permitted to complain. If the authors of the Psalms can shake their fists at the heavens—"my days vanish like smoke,"[14] they write, "how long must your servant wait?"[15]—surely weary parents are invited to be just as honest with God about the difficulties of the day. But even in lament or anger or frustration or flat-out rage, the spiritual discipline of service presses us farther into the hard and worthy work of kingdom-building. When our kids war over a toy or who got a bigger ice cream scoop, we may find ourselves sighing with the psalmist, "too long have I lived among those who hate peace,"[16] but as we fire even our complaints to God, he meets us with understanding and hears us out with compassion and grace.

Service presses us to take a better path than that of the parent-martyr, seeking to serve our kids like Jesus serves us. Washing their dirty faces with love and tenderness; heading into the evening's bath routine with a heart of grace; reading a third bedtime story and answering a thirty-seventh question with patience and courage and care. It may seem an impossible task, but even a step in the right direction brings us closer to the ultimate goal.

Still, I needed to be clear about the bounds of this spiritual discipline. Put another way, if Jesus was mom to my children, how would *he* serve them? Despite, you know, *dying* on the *cross*, Jesus wasn't a martyr in the guilt-trip-grandmother sort of way. Jesus wouldn't say, "You just do whatever *you* want to do. I'm *fine*. I'm just up here *bleeding all over this cross for you*. You go ahead and dump some Matchbox cars in the toilet and smear toothpaste all over the sink. Really. It's all good. I'll just be up here, hanging by the *nails* in my *wrists* and *dying for your sins*." Jesus was a straight-shooter. There was no passive-aggressiveness in him. He wouldn't have survived in my extended family growing up—passive-aggression was how we got things *done*.

I'm also willing to bet Jesus didn't hurry. He wouldn't rush. Jesus would linger for another snuggle with Wilson. He would pause to gently brush the blond hair out of Lincoln's eyes. He would certainly *not* squander those last few moments of parenting in a day by logging on to Facebook. Jesus would notice my husband's exhaustion at the end of six consecutive days of intense ministry, and invite him to go take a walk to the neighborhood hot tub to decompress.

THE EXPERIMENT BEGINS

Month two would be dedicated to the spiritual discipline of service. I would serve Jesus by serving my kids, remembering his words that whatever I do for the least of these—including newborns and preschoolers—I do for him.

But first, a few parameters:

1) **I would seek to practice service specifically at the bedtime hour.** It wasn't that I didn't want to learn to serve Jesus and others at every hour of every day. But hey, *baby steps*.

2) **Serving my kids would not mean doing everything for them.** Like most three-year-olds, sometimes ours struggled to practice basic skills. Having Mom or Dad do things for him was just so much *nicer*! For example, he didn't need help washing his hands, but he often balked at doing it on his own. In those instances, serving him wouldn't be washing his hands *for* him; it would be gently pressing *him* to do it as a way of helping him to grow in maturity. This month's spiritual discipline was servanthood, not enabling.

Jesus models this beautifully. Nowhere in Scripture do we find him running frantically about, attending to the minute needs of everyone in his path. We see him meeting *real* needs—hunger, thirst, healing—and then pressing people to grow in ways they must in order to walk in newness and freedom.

3) **At the bedtime hour, I'd put my phone away.** One hour before the kiddos were slated for lights out on a given night, I would put my phone on the top of our living room bookshelf where I couldn't reach it, see any notifications, or hear any pings.

DAY 1: IF I'M GOING TO RUN THIS MARATHON, I'LL NEED MORE CARBS

I am far from mastering the art of putting two kids to bed simultaneously when they have such different needs. Lincoln is a chatterbox who connects by sharing about his day. Wilson needs silence to nurse to sleep. Linc wants a raucous bath filled with splashing and squirt bottles. Wilson will quite literally drown if enough splashing and squirt bottles are involved in his bath. Handling bedtime alone often feels like a circus act where I'm balanced precariously in a sparkly leotard on the back of a galloping horse, begging the monkeys and elephants to, just this once, be *reasonable*.

But tonight Daryl was home, so we divided and conquered. I nursed Wilson, who faded into sleep with a contented milk-drunk smile. Daryl wrangled Lincoln, who decided to crumple straight to the floor again as soon as Daryl wrapped him in a towel after his bath. Why does he *do* that?

"Ow!" Linc yelled. "I bumped my *face!*" Cue the crying and the Band-Aids and the lavender body lotion that we've convinced him is "medicine" to break him of his Tylenol addiction. (I understand that flavoring kid meds with grape syrup helps kids take them willingly, but *come on*, it also makes our son think he's getting a hit of Kool-Aid.)

We met in Linc's room to read books and snuggle, which was when Wilson woke up. He'd only slept for thirty-five minutes and then started making those happy, "It's morning!" sounds. I peeked into his room, cracking the door just an inch or so, and he popped his little head up like bread from a toaster. This was going to be a long night. At least I had adult company.

DAY 3: IS EXHAUSTION A GOOD EXCUSE?

We sang a song in church this weekend with the lyrics "my flesh and heart may fail." Man, do I feel that these days. No one prepared me for how exhausting motherhood could be. I'm incurably tired almost all the time, and I have two fairly easy kids. No major health problems, no significant behavioral issues. They're three and a half years apart, which means that Lincoln is actually moderately helpful with the baby most days. And yet, I am so tired I put my hair dryer in the laundry hamper yesterday.

My flesh is constantly failing, and some days my will fails me, too. All I want is a long weekend alone and a comfy bed. But that's not the season I'm in. Richard Foster writes that often "ill health or inadequate sleep controls the desire to serve."[17] So basically, as a parent of tiny kids, I may *never* feel like serving. And if I don't feel like it, how will I get it done?

In other news: I cannot—I repeat *cannot*—put my phone away during the bedtime routine for the life of me.

DAY 5: IN WHICH I TOTALLY NAIL IT

I rocked this bedtime routine (she said humbly—I'll work on the sin of pride later, okay?). No phone. Lots of hugs and snuggles. Wilson actually went down twenty minutes before Linc, so Lincoln and I were able to connect over some books and bedtime prayers. He told me he loves me in this deliciously spontaneous three-year-old way, and then tucked his little fingers into my hand and put his head on my shoulder, and I almost died of joy. Why do kids smell so good after their baths? Most of the time he smells like a mixture of potting soil and peanut butter.

I hope that this discipline of service will help me open my eyes to the gift my kids are. You know how older people always look at us young parents and say, "Enjoy every minute!" and we're all, "*I'll cut you*, because you have NO IDEA HOW HARD the last week's worth of minutes has been!" But when I'm not glued to my phone and bedtime goes smoothly, I'm almost drunk with the peacefulness of a sleepy house. Jesus is in this place.

DAY 5 UPDATE: JUST KIDDING

Wilson slept for forty minutes before deciding to wake up and wail for the next *four hours*. This, of course, woke Lincoln up.

He then woke up ten times during the night for various reasons, including but not limited to: "My sock fell off," "I'm afraid there are ladybugs in my bed," and "I missed you."

When will I learn not to count my chickens before they're hatched?

Maybe someday I'll discover what it means to serve my kids with the love and grace and patience of Jesus, when what I really want to do is call my mom to see if she will move in with us forever.

DAY 8: MY CIRCUS, MY MONKEYS

Someone needs to teach me how to get two children to bed anywhere near the same time when one needs to be nursed for twenty minutes in complete darkness and silence and the other one needs an hour-long routine involving a bath, three books, two blankets, socks but no shirt, a prayer, a song, and exactly the right color combination of sippy cup and lid. *This is how people go around the bend and never come back.*

No matter how I endeavor to manage the hour before bedtime, on nights when I'm the solo parent, one kid inevitably ends up screaming or crying or out of his mind. This needs to stop. I can't pay for the therapy bills (for *all* of us) later on; I'm in ministry.

It's not very spiritual of me (and quite possibly heretical), but most of the time I imagine even Jesus couldn't handle both of my kids at bedtime. Back in Jesus' day, didn't most fathers just say to their wives, "The kids are *your* job, woman," and then go out to the carpentry shop or the fishing boat or the fruit stand all day? I see why Catholics love Jesus' mother Mary so much. I want someone who *gets* it, and it's hard to see a single man as my Savior in the throes of young motherhood, because some moments it feels like being a single guy would be so freaking easy. I get that he had to die on a cross in his early thirties, but up until then no one was waking him up at 3 a.m. to tell him they just picked their nose and ate it.

Of course, God has a whole world of crying, toy-throwing, tantrum-having kids (me included) that he cares for patiently and lovingly and mercifully. We, too, refuse to rest when rest is what we need most. But I'll be honest. It's only day eight of this month's experiment, and I don't want to serve my kids anymore. I mean, I'll do what I have to, but I'm not going to have a good attitude about it.

Also, I bet if I sold one of my kidneys on the black market we could afford a night nurse. I'm going to Google it.

DAY 12: PREACHING TO THE PASTOR

One of the best/worst things about being a pastor is that sometimes I'm preparing a sermon for, you know, all those *other* people, and God convicts me. And I'm all like, "Yeah, God, that's fine, but I'm working on a sermon for those *sinners out there*, because I have it all together." And God's all, "Oh right, I forgot. How's that working for you?"

I'm back at the church office this week, fresh from maternity leave, and as I prepared Sunday's sermon, I ran across William Barclay's *Prayers for the Christian Year.* He writes: "Give to your Church preachers and teachers who can make known the Lord Jesus Christ to others because they know him themselves."[18] Daaaaaang, Barclay.

God gave me a little lightbulb moment and gently told me that I've been going about this service experiment from the wrong angle. I can't be Jesus to my kids. Only Jesus can be Jesus.

What I can be is *me*, their mom, the only one they've got…but filled so far up to the brim with Jesus that they get some Jesus through me. Kind of like when I accidentally have too much coffee and it goes into my breast milk and keeps Wilson up all night, but in a good way.

Turns out I've been tending my kids but neglecting my soul, and when I try to be all Jesus-y to them without spending any actual time with Jesus myself, things get super weird super fast. I'm either a holier-than-thou, untouchable angel, this Stepford-Wives-y sort of mom dispensing wisdom and bedtime stories from on high, or I'm a cranky-pants mess who snaps when she should soothe, because my own reservoirs of patience and love have run dry. To serve my kids with the love of Jesus, I have to experience his love for myself. Not just guess at it or try my best to model it, but *know* it deep in my soul.

And to do that, I need to spend some time with him. When, I do not know, because I'm very tired, and there aren't many free minutes in my days. But even if it's a prayer on the fly, I need me some more Jesus.

DAY 14: YOU GOTTA GO DOWN

I always crack up when preachers talk about Jesus' admonitions for us to become like little children because of how innocent and sweet children are. Because: yes, they *are* innocent and sweet, but they are also *handfuls*. I think that's what Jesus is talking about, more than anything: that children have no pretense. They say what they think, they mean what they say, and they go after what they want. Though they are powerless, they are *fierce*.

In Luke 22, Jesus catches his disciples arguing over which one of them will be the greatest. It's a *super* mature argument, and one that has happened countless times since in many a boardroom, mom-gossip circle, and sports arena. The disciples are arguing among themselves when Jesus gently scolds them:

> You are not to be like that. Instead, the greatest among you should be like the youngest, and the one who rules like the one who serves. For who is greater, the one who is at the table or the one who serves? Is it not the one who is at the table? But I am among you as one who serves.[19]

In the topsy-turvy world of the gospel, we have to go down to go up. Edna Hong calls it a "downward ascent."[20] In service, we draw near to the greatest servant of all. It doesn't always make sense. It definitely isn't always easy. But it is deeply and profoundly the way of our God.

DAY 16: HOLY ORDINARY

Daryl was home tonight, praise be. He took Lincoln, who was in full-on crazy-pants mode, and manhandled him into the bathtub, where Linc proceeded to run in place for ten minutes. Because *that's* not dangerous. I envy Daryl's size and strength. Simply picking up both kids and carrying them to the car isn't really an option for me, now that Linc's over thirty pounds and Wilson's nearly twenty. Such heavy lifting is a lot to ask of someone who's not even five and a half feet tall and only three months postpartum.

So Daryl read to Linc while I nursed Wilson on the bed and stroked his downy little head. In those few moments, right before the house falls quiet for the night, I feel heart-exploding love for our little guys. Lincoln is getting *so* big—I can hear him correcting Daryl when Daryl tries to skip a sentence in one of his books—and Wilson is such a jolly little dude, all rolls and grins. It's a gift to have them entrusted to us for this short season, incredibly long as it seems sometimes.

I'm still working through the idea of thinking I need to *be* Jesus to my kids. Sometimes I even ask this of my church, as a pastor: "How can you be Jesus' hands and feet to your neighbor, to our community, to the world?" This remains the wrong question. Jesus is Jesus. His hands and feet belong to *him*. It's not about being Jesus, it's about being *us*—you and me—with our own unique gifts and callings and talents and failings and wants and needs and desires and yes, even hands and feet. My kids desperately need Jesus, but they also need *me*—their mom. How can I be their mom in the deepest, truest way that *I* can be, out of the gifts God has given and the virtue he is working to grow in me? How can I serve them as he serves me?

Maybe that's this month's most profound lesson. That when I'm absolutely at my end, Jesus is waiting to serve me. He's not flagellating me for the ways I didn't quite do the bedtime routine perfectly. He's not shaming me for losing my patience. He's waiting for me to pause for a moment to let him love me, to fill me up so I can be a channel for his love to flow through me to my kids. I don't need to somehow conjure up Jesus' love—it's already there in overwhelming abundance. I just need to let it come in, rushing and gushing and soaking everything in its path.

Thank the Lord, because I simply *cannot* magically drum up that kind of love on my own. I'm learning that, as Karl Rahner put it, "If there is any path at all on which I can approach You [God], it must lead through the very middle of my ordinary daily life."[21] The daily grind has good, hard, beautiful lessons to teach.

DAY 20: REFRESHMENT, PLEASE

I came across a new translation of Matthew 11:28 this week. It's the perhaps familiar to you "Come to me" passage where Jesus speaks to a crowd with great love and tenderness. This translation reads: "Come to me, all you who are weary and find life burdensome, and I will refresh you."[22] It was as if Jesus was looking me straight in the eye and saying, "The bedtime routine is burdensome. I get it. So come to me, and I will fill you up."

I'm not sure how many more reminders I'll need before this sticks, but I'm grateful God keeps offering them.

DAY 24: IS IT ACTUALLY WORKING?

Lincoln: I won't brush my teeth! I will NEVER BRUSH MY TEETH!!!

What I *wanted* to say: Fine. Let them rot out of your head. You'll be the only preschooler with dentures.

What I *actually* said: I know you don't love brushing your teeth, sweetie, but it's just something we have to do.

I hope Jesus smiled. That took some SERIOUS discipline.

DAY 27: SMALL, HARD THINGS

We have decided to start gently sleep training Wilson. He's four months old, so many parenting books say it's okay— including several written by *doctors*—but I still feel like the worst parent in the history of the universe. Okay, maybe second worst, because I'm pretty sure at least Charles Manson has me beat. Did he even have kids? I'm too tired to look it up.

We are sleep training because dear sweet chubby little Wils likes to wake up and eat every hour. And I am beyond zombie-fied. I'm really barely hanging on to my marbles. And he's gone from sweet natured to super cranky, which I imagine is just because he's exhausted, too. So here we are. Tonight when he goes to bed, he won't get to nurse again for a few hours. Daryl will go in and comfort him every few minutes if he cries. I don't know who's going to comfort me.

Sleep training seems to go against the goal of this month—to serve my kids as Jesus would serve them. After all, Jesus gave his very body for us on the cross, didn't he? Then again, Jesus wasn't a pushover. He didn't just do whatever anyone wanted, and he didn't make people happy all the time. Or most of the time, quite honestly. People tried to stone him about as often as they showered him with praise. He told the truth. He loved with a fierce, unyielding, difficult love. A true love. This love wants my baby to sleep so that he can grow and develop and be plugged into the great, big, beautiful world during the day.

You may disagree with me on the sleep thing. Statistically half of you will, and a small percentage of that half will write to tell me that sleep training is coldhearted at best and a breeding ground for psychopathy at worst and that I've probably irreversibly damaged my children. I also feed them boxed macaroni and cheese, if you want to mention that. Tell you what: let's agree to disagree. I'm not an attachment parent; it's just not what has worked for us. Wilsy and I have co-slept on and off, but now that he's a wiggle worm, it's impossible *and* dangerous (wrought-iron headboard entanglement, anyone?), so here we are.

Sigh. I'm dreading tonight. Being a parent is too hard. I'm going to quit, move to Liberia, and herd goats. But only adult ones.

DAY 29: A LEGIT MIRACLE

Wilson sleeps for five hours at a stretch now. It's freaking *awesome*. I find myself singing upbeat tunes from *Les Misérables* to him and anyone within earshot every morning because I'm bursting with energy and happiness. During the day he's back to his chipper little self; he coos and sings and snuggles. Want to know how long he cried the first night? Twenty minutes. Daryl went in to comfort him every few minutes. Then the little guy slept like a baby (ha) for five hours. I feel like an idiot for putting this off so long, and a bigger idiot for dreading it.

Uncertain acts of service—drawing boundaries, taking risks, stepping into uncharted waters—are acts of faith, too, and I'm so thankful for the ways God has met our little family with sleep this week. Cheers for rest. Cheers for a God who, as the psalmist writes, "grants sleep to those he loves."[23] Hallelujah. Amen.

DAY 31: I AM WEAK, BUT HE IS STRONG

Bedtime is hard, you guys, but this month has been so good. Not because it's been easy, but because I've begun to realize that God is present at my lowest moments. He doesn't swoop in and make it all magically simple or joy-filled (or even seemingly possible some nights), but he is there. As the wise and winsome Kate Bowler puts it in *Everything Happens for a Reason*, "What if being people of 'the gospel' meant that we are simply people with good news? God is here. We are loved. It is enough."[24]

I think part of me expected this month's experiment in service to give me more answers, more strength, more ease with the difficult parts of parenting. Instead it's given me increasing knowledge of my own human frailty and of the grace of a God who keeps showing up in the midst of the mess. And today that is more than enough.

JOIN THE JOURNEY

What is the most difficult part of your parenting day? Consider how you might serve your kids during that hour. For me it was the bath and bedtime routine. If your kids are older, it may be the dinnertime routine, getting them out the door for school in the morning, or even long car rides to sports practices.

Seek to serve them alongside Jesus—you don't have to become Jesus, but instead use the unique gifts he's given you to serve with his love flowing through you. I'd encourage you to put your phone and screens away so you can serve more intentionally during that hour.

The following passages of Scripture may help to aid you in your service:

Luke 9:48
Luke 22:24–27
Romans 12:3
Galatians 5:13

CHAPTER 4

EATING & THE EXAMEN
Finding God at the Dinner Table

*The oldest form of theater is the dinner table
…new show every night, same players.*
—Michael J. Fox

Dinnertime is one of the best times of day at our house. Everyone is quiet and still, at least for a few moments. We get the chance to look each other in the eye, to sit down, to spend some time coming back together after church and work and preschool and all of the hustle of the previous hours. Dinnertime is sacred. Even on the days we eat in the In-N-Out drive-thru or one of us speeds off afterward for an evening meeting, it is a holy hour.

It doesn't always *feel* holy to take care of our bodily needs though, does it? I'll be the first to admit that segmenting life into two separate categories—"spiritual work" and "everything else"—is all too tempting. Praying before bed? Spiritual. Washing the dishes? Everything else. Going to church? Spiritual. Eating dinner in the midst of a cranky preschooler, an overtired infant, and a rushed husband who is running late for a meeting? So. Not. Spiritual. Right?

But God loves tangible things. He created the material world, after all, from microscopic cells to whopping whales, from red, hot lava to cool, clean water. God is in the business of the *real*. Yet all too often I place God solely in the spiritual realm. My soul might be for God, but my body, calendar, mind, heart, bank account, family—these are for *me*.

It's a tempting separation. After all, if God is relegated to the spiritual realm, we are in charge of all the rest. God can have all the ethereal, unreal, religious feelies, we reason. We will handle the physical stuff.

Yet the first two months of spiritual disciplines landed me right in the middle of this dichotomy. Contemplation felt vaporous—something that happened only in the spiritual realm. God was present, of course, but practicing contemplation while I drove often seemed to remove me from being fully available to my family. Serving them was a good exercise, and one that taught me a great deal, but it was also between God and me, and though my family reaped many of the benefits, they weren't really in on the process.

I needed to ground this month's spiritual discipline right in the middle of the boots-on-the-ground, tangible, physical real world. It was time for the Examen.

The Examen is a spiritual practice that dates back to St. Ignatius of Loyola and his particular subset of monks known as Jesuits. Ignatius taught that God calls believers to lives of service, so Jesuits were often a people on the go. This contrasted with other monastics like the Benedictines, who tended to be a more contemplative, rooted sort. Knowing how busy his adherents' lives were, Ignatius came up with a spiritual exercise they could do in the midst of their eventful, fast-paced lives, to help keep them connected to God. Despite never marrying or having children, Ignatius really seemed to get the whole speed-of-family-life thing. Bless him.

THE EXAMEN
INSPECTING THE HOURS OF OUR DAYS BEFORE GOD—OUR UPS AND DOWNS, SUCCESSES AND FAILURES, GRACES AND SINS.

INVITING GOD TO HELP US BECOME MORE AWARE OF HOW HIS PRESENCE IS WITH US THROUGHOUT THE DAY.

The exercise is called "The Examen," named so because it's the practice of examining your day in order to notice God's presence in its events. Say you took your child, suffering from an ear infection, to the pediatrician, where you discovered that the wait time was shorter than normal. At the day's end, as you think back over the surprisingly short wait and the blessing of seeing a doctor and receiving treatment, you might thank God for his presence in providing health care, shortening a wait, and getting your child the help she needed.

Since my previous spiritual exercises were done with my family present but largely without their knowledge, I wanted this month to be something we could do together. Or at least my husband, Linc, and me, since four-month-old Wilson wasn't exactly verbal yet. (I'm pretty sure if he *was* verbal he'd mostly just alternate between yelling, "More MILLLLLLK!" and "I hate this car seat with the fire of a thousand suns!")

THE JOURNEY BEGINS

At its simplest, the Examen is just looking at some of the day's moments and searching for God in their midst. As Kevin O'Brien notes, "St. Ignatius believed that we can find God in all things, at every moment, even in the most ordinary times."[25] Since kids need a narrower framework than "every moment," Daryl and I decided to focus on finding God in one difficult/low moment and one awesome/high moment every day. Each night at dinner we would take turns sharing our low and high and where we noticed God in those events.

Simple, right?

Because we were usually together for dinner, we would tie our Examen to eating. For one meal a day, we'd bring Jesus in amid the plastic Lightning McQueen dishes, garlicky chicken, spilled milk, refused vegetables, and constant requests for dessert. Because you can't get more creaturely than talking about Jesus while putting food in your gullet.

DAY 1: THE PRESCHOOLER AND THE PHD

At our first Examen meal, almost-four-year-old Lincoln shared that his high was singing to music in the car with me. (Awwwww.) His low was when he fell and scraped his knee. He seemed to be grasping the concept right off the bat, which made my pastor's heart well up with pride.

"What was your low?" I asked Daryl. He glanced nervously at Lincoln.

"Um…how specific do you want me to get?"

"Preschooler appropriate."

"Well…there was a *person* who sort of made things difficult today…"

"Who?" chirped Lincoln. Daryl eyed me. We can't name drop around Lincoln anymore because he repeats *everything* to *everyone*.

"Just a person," said Daryl. "And he-or-she made things difficult because he-or-she came into the office and…Oh, this isn't working."

"Pick a different thing," I said.

"But THIS was my low!" he protested. I married a literalist.

DAY 3: IN WHICH LINCOLN REALIZES HE CAN USE THE EXAMEN TO BEG FOR THEME PARK TICKETS

"My low was not getting to go to Legoland," Lincoln said on our third day of the Examen, his face downcast, his eyes welling up with crocodile tears. We hadn't talked about Legoland in months. Going to Legoland wasn't a *thing*.

"What was the best part of your day?" I asked.

"Well," he said, "I think the best part of my day was how God helped me believe that maybe I can go to Legoland tomorrow." Turns out Lincoln is pretty savvy and quickly discovered that he could turn his prayer requests into thinly veiled pleas for stuff he wanted.

"Anything else?" I asked.

"Nope. That's it."

DAY 5: THE STORIES WE TELL

Daryl and I were slowly learning to be patient with Lincoln as we modeled our own lows. We also gradually stopped trying to interpret his day for him after I assumed the thirty-minute tantrum that resulted in multiple time-outs would be a low, but instead he talked about not getting to go see Mickey Mouse. His thirty-minute tantrum was certainly *my* low.

The Examen had begun to teach me to let my son tell his own unique story. It started helping him connect with God in his own way, teaching me to trust that God would faithfully show up in his day, just as he did in mine.

DAY 8: PATIENCE, AND OTHER THINGS I LACK

I didn't imagine the Examen would be such a school for patience, but I suppose Ignatius didn't practice it with a preschooler.

"What was your high today?" I asked Lincoln a week into the experiment. He'd started to get the hang of things.

"Being with Daddy at the park."

"That's awesome! Let's thank God for that!"

"Thanks for the park, God!" said Lincoln. "And thanks for Daddy!" My heart began swelling with pride. Our son was finding Jesus in the midst of his day! He was *getting it*!

"What was your low?" I asked.

"Well, I think it was when I was underwater and all the sharks were coming. Even the baby sharks."

"Ah…yes," I paused to shoot eye-daggers at Daryl, who was trying unsuccessfully to keep from chuckling, "well, that *would* be a low now, wouldn't it?"

DAY 11: DINNERTIME SEMINARY

Tonight my high was that Wilson's tear duct finally opened. A closed or clogged tear duct is a common problem in newborns, and it isn't serious, painful, or contagious, but until the duct opens it results in a crusty, yellow, goopy mess that needs to be cleaned regularly. My niece Sophia asked why we put guacamole in his eye. It really was pretty gross. The worst bit was that Wilson *hated* the whole warm-compresses-and-massage we had to perform on him upwards of six times a day.

"I'm so thankful Jesus healed Wilson," I said. Linc took this in between bites of chicken and glares at asparagus.

"Does God always heal us?" he asked. A long pause ensued. Daryl and I each grew up going to church. We attended a flagship Christian college. I spent three years in seminary, and Daryl is nearly finished with his PhD in theology. I've been in ordained ministry for eight years and Daryl for four. We are continually stumped by the theological questions of our preschooler.

"Well, yes," I said. "God is the great healer. Sometimes we get better right away. Other times it takes a while. And sometimes God doesn't heal us until we're with him in heaven. But we can always pray and ask him for healing."

"Oh," he said, his blue eyes boring deeply into mine. He paused. "Can I have dessert?"

DAY 14: THE GOD WHO HEALS

Lincoln peeled off a two-day-old Band-Aid from a cut on his finger and peered at the wound curiously.

"I'm better!" he chirped, happily. Then he looked at the ceiling. "That's the best part of my day. Thanks, Jesus!"

While we washed the dinner dishes (or, let's be honest, dumped the pizza boxes into the recycling bin…), Daryl and I shared the sweetly mundane highs and lows of our day. UCLA won their football game; my hair had finally grown long enough to fit into a ponytail; the garbage ripped and spilled chicken guts onto the floor; I was ten minutes late to the class I teach because of a traffic jam. In the holy ordinary, standing on the cold tile of the kitchen floor, we met God and he met us.

The push to name God's presence in the everyday was a constant challenge for us both, but as the month wore on, we began to see him everywhere. We started to notice God in the carpool lane, at the office, during the porch discussion with a neighbor, amid the grapes and cherries in the produce section, as we locked up the house for the night. Watching, waiting, blessing, helping. Granting strength. Giving hope. Breathing life. The Examen woke us up to his presence. He was there all along, but only now had we begun to see.

DAY 22: TUNING IN

If we ever forget to start the Examen at dinnertime, Lincoln reminds us. He has begun to love our nightly practice, the chance to reflect on his day. Noticing God's presence in the ordinary moments seems to come much more naturally to him than it does to Daryl and me.

I'm often surprised by which moments made an impression on each of us. Moments I barely noticed are seared in Lincoln's memory. Moments that washed over me stuck with Daryl. Moments the boys didn't notice shaped my whole day. We are noticing God at work more often, but we are also beginning to learn about one another—what bugs, encourages, frustrates, or inspires each of us. The church doesn't often talk about how drawing closer to God brings us closer to one another, but we should; it's profoundly true.

I'm also struck by how much of the Christian faith centers on awareness. No wonder God commanded his people in the early Old Testament to bind his commandments on their foreheads, to write them on the doorposts of their homes. We are a forgetful people. The Examen reminds.

DAY 25: THE BEAUTY OF PAIN

In his *Letters from the Desert,* Carlo Carretto writes:

> Jesus…taught us to live every hour of the day as saints. Every hour of the day is useful and may lead to divine inspiration, the will of the Father, the prayer of contemplation—holiness. Every hour of the day is holy. What matters is to live it as Jesus taught us. And for this one does not have to shut oneself in a monastery or fix strange and inhumane regimes for one's life. It is enough to accept the realities of life. Work is one of those realities; motherhood, the rearing of children, family life with all its obligations are others.[26]

The Examen, simple as our version of it is, is helping me to see that each hour of the day truly is holy. God is in and through each hour, each minute, every second that ticks away.

Processing our nightly highs and lows as a family is teaching me daily that God is present in both. That he brings blessing and joy, but he's found in the pain, too. In church this Sunday we sang a verse of Elizabeth Prentiss's gorgeous and haunting hymn "More Love to Thee, O Christ":

> Let sorrow do its work, come grief or pain;
> Sweet are Thy messengers, sweet their refrain,
> When they can sing with me: More love, O Christ, to Thee;
> More love to Thee, more love to Thee!

I'll admit that I expected God to show up in the good things, but I'm surprised to find him just as evident in the difficult ones. Tonight the Examen brought out my fear of failing as a writer and Daryl's frustration with a season of unexpected frailty as he recovered from knee surgery. God didn't remove the pain or the fear, but instead sat with us in their midst, offering his presence, his comfort, his love.

Of course, kids face pain, too. "My low was when Audrey got hurt at school," Linc told us. Audrey's his best friend, and he's her self-appointed playground guardian. "She fell on the slide and scraped her knee, and she was sad and I was sad." We paused, waiting for him to continue. "God made her better," he said. "Well, God and Miss Misty, who gave her a cold sponge."

DAY 31: THE EXAMEN REMAINS

Our month's experiment is ended, but we plan to keep this family practice going. It's folded seamlessly into our family life, a daily reminder of God at work. Plus, it's helpful to have a set ritual for the dinner hour besides haggling with the preschooler over vegetables. It's brought Daryl and me into a deeper awareness of God in the lives of our children, too—how and where they see him. This month has been a win. I think Ignatius would be proud.

JOIN THE JOURNEY

The Examen is an ancient spiritual practice centered in remembering our day and looking for God's presence within it. We chose dinnertime to do the Examen; you may wish to pick the same time, another meal, bedtime, or whatever hour your family is most likely to be together. We found it helpful to give our son free reign in what he shared. As we modeled our highs and lows, eventually he stopped asking for toys and trips to Disneyland and began sharing from his heart. And also his imagination. It was an adventure for sure.

The following Scriptures may help you as you pursue the Examen:

Psalm 27
Psalm 139
Jeremiah 17:10
Matthew 6:1–15
Philippians 3:13–14

CHAPTER 5

LAUNDRY & LISTENING PRAYER

Because Sometimes the Voice of God Sounds a Lot like the Dryer

My sheep listen to my voice.
—Jesus, John 10:27

Early in our marriage, it was decided that Daryl would handle the laundry. And by "it was decided," I mean that *Daryl* decided, because I did a few loads in our first newlywed days and turned a bunch of his white undershirts pink, and we were on a super-tight budget, so they couldn't be replaced for months. I may have shrunk his favorite dress shirt, too; I don't really remember because I have mild PTSD from the argument that ensued where he accused me of *being in a hurry* and *not paying enough attention*, and I explained to him that he needn't be so *fussy*, the items in question were just *pieces of clothing*, not the Hope Diamond. We fought a lot early in our marriage, and by "fought" I don't mean civilized discussion, I mean yelling at each other from opposite ends of an eight-hundred-square-foot apartment during Chicago winters that were too cold to take our tiffs outside where they could benefit from distance and fresh air.

So anyway, Daryl does the wash.

He separates colors and makes sure we're stocked with detergent and is intimately acquainted with our washer and dryer. He drops off the dry cleaning and does the ironing when there is ironing to be done. My one and only laundry-related job is to fold and put away. That's it. Small potatoes, really, in the supermarket of laundry.

But here's the thing: I *don't* fold it. Or put it away. I mean, I do *sometimes*, but those sometimes-times are bi-monthly at best, so the rest of the time we end up living out of laundry baskets like college students and wearing rumpled jeans that wouldn't be so rumpled if I had actually taken twenty seconds to fold them and put them into a drawer where they belong.

Daryl says very little about this. I married well.

Another thing: well over eighteen months have passed in our lives between the last chapter of this book and this one. I took a break both from the book and from pressing into specific spiritual disciplines, because life happened. We moved, faced some health issues, and ramped up programs at church. Another writing project was due; the kids needed to see a bit more of us; we needed a season of rest. This may happen to you, too. If it does, come back to the disciplines when you can, without guilt. Sometimes these interruptions are God's grace, given so we have time to digest the previous spiritual practices. Contemplation takes time. Service is something we'll always be growing into more fully. The Examen is meant to be a lifelong pattern. No shame. There is always a new day to begin again.

So now our older son is five, and our younger is nearly two, and they are both in the business of getting incredibly dirty all day every day, and laundry hill has turned into laundry mountain, and I'm still doing next to no folding and putting away. I could give you all sorts of theological reasons ordinary household tasks are important not only for the home economy but for the soul, and I genuinely believe them all, but also I am lazy, and at the end of a long day the last thing I want to do is fold socks. Or pray, to be completely honest.

Enter: listening prayer.

Adele Calhoun calls listening prayer a practice that allows "God to set the agenda."[27] For Henri Nouwen, listening is "the real work" of prayer.[28] The idea behind listening prayer is that we quiet our minds and hearts so we can hear God speak to us. We speak to him, too, but then we leave long silences, waiting for his response, his guidance, assurances of his love. If you think about it, listening prayer makes a lot of sense. God speaks—through Scripture, through circumstance, through creation, through friends—but we must leave room to hear from him.

LISTENING PRAYER
QUIETING OURSELVES TO LISTEN TO THE STILL, SMALL VOICE OF GOD AND PONDERING THE WORDS THAT WE RECEIVE IN THE LIGHT OF SCRIPTURE.

Up until this point in parenthood, my prayer life had been pretty ad hoc. Daryl and I prayed with the kids before meals and at bedtime. I prayed over major decisions and as I struggled to get out of bed in the early morning. Together we pray for the needs of our congregation, our friends, our families. God wasn't a stranger, but my prayer life lacked intentionality, regularity, dedication. My desire was that this month would help change that, turning me from a pray-when-the-mood-strikes type of conversation partner with God to one who followed Paul's call to "pray without ceasing."[29] I hoped that tying prayer to a chore I needed to do anyway would make it inescapable, inevitable, guaranteed.

My dad used to do all the laundry folding in my childhood home, in part because then he had an excuse to watch the Green Bay Packers on TV, but also because as he folded each item of clothing, he'd pray for us. That my two sisters and I would know our worth in Christ. That we'd grow up to love and serve him. That we wouldn't go off and marry the first guy with a truck who asked us on a date. (That was a close call for one of us, but I won't say whom.)

Laundry is intimate. Our clothes get dirty with all the matters of our days—dirt and food, sweat and tears, blood and spit-up. Our washing machine broke back when I was only a few weeks postpartum with Wilson, and Daryl was just two days past his knee surgery. I'd forgotten how much laundry babies made— veritable bushels of laundry, like it's their *job*—and I was fast approaching despair. My friend Eva called out of the blue and said, "Heard your washing machine broke. I'm coming over. Give me all your laundry."

My first thought was, *awesome.* My second, following on its heels within nanoseconds, was, *Oh, dear God, I cannot give her our laundry.* I'd gained upwards of fifty pounds in this pregnancy, and the last thing I wanted was a dear friend glimpsing what I'd been referring to as my "wind-sail panties." That combined with the fact that I'd been leaking all manner of everything onto my clothing since Wilson was born (no one tells you that you and your baby *both* go home in a diaper after birth…), and I couldn't have possibly been more ashamed of those baskets of laundry.

"What *are* you doing?" Daryl asked, watching me hastily snatch pieces of clothing from the baskets and stash them in a spare basket in our bedroom.

"I'm taking out all the underwear," I said.

"Court, we need clean underwear. It's not like Eva's going to *examine* it before she puts it in her washing machine."

"I'm not taking yours out," I said. "Just mine."

Eva arrived and popped her trunk, carrying basket after basket down to her SUV.

"Thank you," I said, tears in my eyes. The days immediately postpartum are quite a school for humility. She hugged me, and as she did, glimpsed something over my shoulder.

"What's that?" she asked, pointing to the corner of our bedroom where I'd built a leaning tower of unmentionables in our one remaining basket. Obviously suffering from postpartum sleep delirium, I managed to muster up enough initiative to take *out* the underwear from the main laundry baskets, but not enough to actually put them somewhere that would successfully escape Eva's gaze. Eva's a lawyer—she doesn't miss a *thing*.

"Oh that's..." I said, scrambling for a reasonable explanation.

"Looks like laundry!" she chirped, scooping it up and heading out the door. My cheeks burned crimson. Daryl burst into laughter. Not only did Eva have my dirty laundry, now *she had an entire basket of just my underwear.*

Like my dear friend who could be fully trusted with my messiest secrets, God meets us in these intimate, bodily, human places. As Tish Harrison Warren writes in *The Liturgy of the Ordinary*, "God entered all of it. He did not shrink back from Adam and Eve's shame. Instead, he covered it."[30] Laundry is a constant reminder of our bodilyness, our close ties to the material world. God meets us in these physical places, the sacred tangible.

I've often viewed folding the laundry as a burdensome chore because I've decided I have more important things to do. But Jesus spoke of sparrows and mustard seeds and lost coins; surely my overflowing plastic baskets weren't far from his light. God wanted to speak to me in the midst of those piles of shirts and pants and socks. The question was: Would I listen?

THE JOURNEY BEGINS

For this spiritual exercise, I gave myself a few simple guidelines.

1) **I'd kneel before and after, as a physical reminder of what I was about to do.** To our own detriment, Protestants often shy away from anything overly physical in worship, turning our faith into a mental exercise rather than a holistic one that necessarily includes the body. This is, quite simply, wrong. Our bodies need to pray, too. As we train them, they will help train us, opening the door to the Spirit of prayer and creating conditions where our souls turn to it more regularly and naturally. So I'd kneel first and afterward, to mark the time.

2) **I'd let the laundry itself help guide my prayers.** If I was folding things belonging to Wilson, I'd hold him before the Lord in prayer and listen. The same would be true for Lincoln, Daryl, and me.

That was it. I was ready. Too bad I hadn't folded any clothes in about three weeks. Laundry Everest awaited.

DAY 1: I'M NO MOUNTAIN CLIMBER

I planned to fold laundry during the boys' naps today, but I put it off so I could read and nap and watch a YouTube video on how to tape a sprained ankle (a legitimate need), and also Nancy Kerrigan's freestyle skating program from the 1996 Olympics (in no way a legitimate need), and then, of course, Wilson woke up. So I brought him into our bedroom where we now had four unfolded baskets of laundry, because I clearly suffer from some sort of deep-seated fear of performing mundane household tasks, and I started in on the project.

Wilson is at an age where he's curious about anything I'm doing, so he dragged over his little step stool and sat on it and watched me for several minutes. I prayed as I folded, asking God for energy for Daryl, who is worn down because he's a dad and a pastor, and both involve quite a bit of heavy lifting. I listened for Jesus and I folded and I watched Wilson, who watched me.

I don't look at my kids very much. I *mind* them, of course. I keep them alive and cook them dinner and take them to school and the park and the doctor, but I don't often just gaze at them. I watched his rosy cheeks, still flushed from his nap, and the way the hair at the back of his neck curled, and he met my gaze and smiled with the jack-o'-lantern smile of a toddler who only has seven teeth, and then he laughed.

Without the laundry, I would have been on the move from the moment he woke up. I'm thankful for the space to listen not only to Jesus but to my son today.

DAY 3: THE FAITHFUL MUNDANE

Yes, there's still laundry to do. Yes, Daryl and I had a heated moment this morning because he asked me if I'd fold and put the kids' clothes away because their drawers were basically empty, but he asked before 9 a.m. on a Saturday and I was *so not having that kind of talk*. (I'm super fun to be married to.)

Then he left for lunch with a friend, and I'm at home staring down five baskets overflowing with laundry. I literally didn't even know we owned five laundry baskets.

Psalm 85 was with me this afternoon. "I listen carefully to what God the LORD is saying, for he speaks peace to his faithful people."[31] Listening has become something of a lost art. I can think of a few friends who truly listen well—fully dialed in, eyes focused, no distracting pings or tweets. Those minutes together with them are a gift. I want to learn to listen to God in this same way. For the sake of my soul *and* my marriage, I'm glad this is the spiritual discipline of the month.

As I folded, I realized quickly that a lot of the laundry was mine. Nursing tank tops and work blouses, pajama pants sporting llamas on them (don't judge, you know you're just jealous), jeans that accidentally went through the dryer and now, barring the stomach flu, will never fit me again. I breathed in and out. I offered myself to God. There were no epiphanies. No come-to-Jesus moments. But I felt myself loved, and the laundry got put away, and those two small miracles were the whole world.

DAY 6: LISTENING FRIENDSHIP

My friend Annie came over today. Our older kids were in school, so our two youngers played together while we tackled laundry folding. It wasn't premeditated; I just started folding a couple of shirts while we talked—the kids had wandered into the room where the laundry was—and she quickly joined in.

"Is it okay if I...?" she asked, pointing to a basket of socks.

"Go for it," I said. Annie is the type of friend who thanks you for letting her help with your laundry. The world needs more Annies.

As we folded, I listened to her and she listened to me, and we talked about what God is teaching us, the ups and downs of what had been a particularly hard week for us both. Our time together was, I think, its own kind of listening prayer.

DAY 10: HOLY SILENCES

Former CBS anchor Dan Rather once asked Mother Teresa what she talked to God about. "I don't say anything. I listen," she replied.

"What is it that God says to you when you pray?" he asked.

"He also doesn't talk. He simply listens," she said.[32]

There is something incredibly sacred about holding a silence in a word-filled world. Most often in my laundry folding, I haven't heard anything from God. There have been no huge breakthroughs yet, and to be honest, I'm not really expecting any. But there has been holy silence. God is present, and in keeping silent, I more easily remember that he is there, and become more ready to welcome him. I am present, arm-deep in socks and shirts (nearly all of them striped—*why* are so many little boy shirts striped?). I hold the silence open for God and let my spirit rest in him, and he holds that same silence open for me.

I'm no Mother Teresa, but she was really on to something.

DAY 18: I MARRIED WELL

Daryl ended up folding the rest of the laundry this week. All of it. A bushel's worth. He didn't complain, but I still feel guilty. He takes the lead on a lot of the house stuff when my plate fills with other things—writing and kid appointments and church initiatives. He does it silently, willingly, kindly. In our marriage

I'm sometimes the squeaky wheel, and he's the Clydesdale that pulls the cart with the squeaky wheel.

No one tells you when you start dating in your twenties that you should look for someone kind enough to fold all the laundry without asking, and that marrying that person will make you infinitely happier than marrying the person with the best abs.

DAY 22: TOO MUCH, TOO FAST?

I'm realizing that it was overambitious of me to add in *two* disciplines this month. It's one thing to tie a spiritual practice to a task I already do on a regular basis—driving, meals, bath time. It's something else completely to take on a household task I hate and dread while also adding a spiritual discipline to it. In other words, I haven't been folding any laundry this week, so I also haven't been practicing listening prayer. And now I feel guilty about both.

Still, in a beautiful biblical paradox of sorts, in these low moments I've begun to be encouraged. As Ole Hallesby notes, in his deep and delightful book *Prayer*,

> As far as I can see, prayer has been ordained only for the helpless. It is the last resort of the helpless. Indeed, the very last way out. We try everything before we finally resort to prayer....Prayer and helplessness are inseparable. Only those who are helpless can truly pray.[33]

The previous months of spiritual disciplines have started to teach me a sort of divine resilience borne out of my own ineptitude. Seeking Jesus and falling short is *normal*. The first step is embracing the helplessness that becomes exposed when we fall short. I *cannot* follow Jesus faithfully. I simply can't. I lack the willpower, the strength, the character—even, some days, the very desire. Yet in standing exposed before God, stripped of my pretensions and pretending, my metaphorical Spanx no longer holding in the places I'm ashamed of, I'm finally ready to fall into the arms of Jesus and let him minister his grace to me. The first step is simply holding open my empty hands so he can fill them back up, not as a reward for good-girl behavior that's fallen short once again, but out of his deep love for me even so. When we miss a day or a month or ten years of prayer—when we disobey, turn away, or simply run out of steam—God is there. Gracious, merciful, and ever ready to welcome and help us press in again.

"You know," Father Cosmás says to poet Scott Cairns, "once you've begun, you need only continue. Prayer will come."[34] So much of practicing spiritual disciplines is simply showing up once more. Whether it is after a long hiatus—as it was for me between the last chapter and this one—or the very next morning, God greets us with open arms. Neither God nor we gain anything from wallowing in sorrow or self-pity. If we've been away, God invites us back. If we've been consistent, our soul-muscles will grow stronger, but we never become invincible. The work of God is always grace. When we show up, in whatever capacity, in whatever state we find ourselves, it's there.

DAY 30: YIELDING TO GRACE

I am still very bad at laundry, but I feel a good bit more comfortable in listening prayer. It's as if the past few days and weeks have begun to teach me to be patient with silences, paying attention to what is within and outside of me. Inconsistent as I've been with this household chore, the gift of listening prayer is that it doesn't require anything but silence and attentiveness. Granted, those are both very difficult things to offer up at times, but they are two things that belong to each of us. Two things all of us can give, if sometimes only in fits and starts.

Listening prayer is a form of surrender, of giving up control, of allowing the Spirit to lead and guide and talk and listen. So much of prayer isn't doing but waiting, resting, giving up control to the only one who is provident over all. André Louf, in *Teach Us to Pray*, writes, "There comes a moment when we yield up God's Word to the Spirit within us. Then it is that our heart gives birth to prayer."[35]

Laundry may never be my bailiwick. Daryl and I are already in conversations to swap a few household responsibilities so I can prepare more meals and he can take over the laundry entirely. (Can you *hear* the hallelujahs?) But listening prayer can be practiced anywhere quiet enough that tuning in to the Spirit of God is possible. I see fewer podcasts in my future and lots of prayerful cooking. I can't wait.

JOIN THE JOURNEY

Choose a quiet household chore—for me it was laundry, but perhaps you are the primary dishwasher in your family, or floor sweeper, or shelf duster, or bathroom scrubber. Invite God into those times by turning off your devices, quieting your heart, and listening for him. I found it helpful to kneel before and after to mark off the time and help teach my body alongside my soul. If you find your mind wandering as you learn to listen to God (and believe me, you will!), let the chore before you be your guide.

Check what you hear against the biblical witness. If you hear things that contradict what you know to be true of Scripture, bring them to a pastor or wise Christian friend to talk them through. I've found that God most often speaks to me of kindness, affirmation, challenge, and conviction—the same things I regularly find when reading Scripture. But on the occasions I'm not sure whether I'm sensing something from God, my own ego, or the burrito I ate hours earlier that isn't agreeing well with me, I bring the questions to Scripture and to others I trust to help me confirm or dispel them.

Be patient with yourself. Developing the practice of listening prayer is a lifelong process, and God's voice is often subtle. It will take time to tune in.

The following Scriptures may help guide you in your listening prayer journey:

1 Samuel 1:15	John 10:27
Luke 18:1	John 14:13
John 7:16	Acts 9:1–19

CHAPTER 6

SHOWERING WITH SCRIPTURE
Wash over Me, Lord

*The word of Scripture should never stop sounding
in your ears and working in you all day long,
just like the words of someone you love.*
—Dietrich Bonhoeffer

Some days the only time I spend completely by myself is during my shower. When our boys were tiny, I'd buckle them into a bouncy seat right outside the shower curtain and take a few blissful minutes to wash away the stains of the day alone— or as alone as I could possibly be in those first few weeks of parenthood. Lincoln would usually coo and kick his legs happily. Wilson fluctuated between raging and napping. Either way, I savored those fleeting minutes when it was just me and some cheap shampoo and Dr. Bronner's Peppermint Soap sudsing up to get a clean start on the day's work.

No one tells you before you have kids that a simple shower could grow to be so precious. Pre-kid, most of us have quite a bit of time to ourselves. Driving to work, sleeping in on a Saturday, going to the bathroom. Post-kid, nearly every activity is shared. I mentioned this to my friend Jeff when he and his wife were expecting their first child. He's the most introverted person I've ever met, and he paled visibly.

"That's going to take some...getting used to," he said.

And it does. I am not too spiritual to admit that I miss certain things about my unencumbered life before kids. I miss sleeping in on Saturdays, being able to run into a store for a quick errand without unbuckling the equivalent of two NASA shuttle safety harnesses, having uninterrupted thoughts while cooking dinner, and doing the *New York Times* crossword puzzle without someone "helping" in crayon. But I definitely miss using the bathroom alone the most. We rarely even shut the bathroom door at our house these days, since a closed door is basically a toddler's invitation to come in and join the party. Sometimes, if I am very, very quick, I can do my business alone, and in those moments, I come out of the bathroom feeling like a Super Ninja. Amazing what feels like a victory in the throes of parenthood.

I miss using the restroom solo more than anything, but spending time alone with Jesus, my Bible, and a warm beverage? That's a close second. Some of my friends still manage to take a precious half hour before the kids wake up for the day to be alone with Jesus. I salute them; I really do. But my youngest regularly rises before 5 a.m., and there is no way I'm spiritual enough to have anything resembling quality time with the Almighty before it's light outside. I'm just not a morning person; it takes me a good hour and two cups of coffee before I even approach approachability. Anyone relate?

The college I attended demolished its singles' breakfast bar my junior year—the one place in the cafeteria I could grab a bowl of Lucky Charms and not have to speak to another living soul. I know they were trying to encourage "community" or whatever, but the reality is that I never went to breakfast there again. During our first years of marriage, Daryl was working on a PhD, using those early morning hours to hole up in a coffee shop where he'd pound out his coursework and, later, his dissertation. We rarely saw each other before 9 a.m. After he graduated, he was around in the early mornings for the first time, and he asked me the same two questions for three straight months:

"Is everything okay? Did I say something that's bothering you?"

I'd answer it the same way each day: "You're not bothering me; being *awake* is bothering me." Apparently my normal morning face tells passersby that I might commit homicide.

So morning time with Jesus was out, once kids arrived on the scene. But that meant I'd put off spending time in Scripture until I was preparing to head to bed at the end of the day, and those moments between holding my toothbrush and crawling into bed were the only moments that approached the same exhaustion I'd faced in the pre-coffee moments of the day. So, needless to say, it didn't happen then, either.

STUDYING SCRIPTURE
DEVOTING TIME AND ATTENTION
TO THE WORDS OF THE BIBLE.

SEEKING TO UNDERSTAND ITS CONTEXT, MEANING,
CULTURE, HISTORY, AND PERSONAL APPLICATIONS.

I *wanted* to spend time with Jesus; I just had no earthly idea where to fit it in on an average day. I remained intimate with Scripture because I led Bible studies and prepared sermons at church, but my own spiritual life suffered from neglect. So I'd feel terrible—bad Christian, bad pastor, bad mom. I wasn't just driven by shame, either. I *wanted* more time in Scripture. Reading through the Bible, journaling questions and doubts and verses that struck me, knitting these ancient words into the fabric of my modern existence—this was water to my parched soul. I didn't just feel like I *should* do it; my heart longed for it. I wanted to "plant the Word of God so soberly and so deeply" in my heart, as Bonhoeffer wrote, that it would "hold and strengthen" me "all day long, leading … to active love, to obedience, to good works."[36] The longer I spent away from the Bible, or just dabbling in it here and there, the thirstier I grew. There *had* to be a way to drink deeply from the Word of God without setting an alarm for 4:30 a.m.

Then it hit me—what if I *showered* with Scripture?

THE JOURNEY BEGINS

Daryl's on an organizing kick. He's purchased tons of whiteboards and dry erase markers. Turns out you can use these to draw on shower tile, too. (Don't take my word for it—check it on a small, unobtrusive area of your own before complaining that you ruined expensive granite. We have cheap subway tile that wipes off clean as a whistle!) I'm going to write a verse or two a day in the shower and let the word of God soak me from head to toe in the few naturally solitary moments of my day.

DAY 1: MY SHOWER DOESN'T COME IN BRAILLE

If I don't put my contacts in before showering, all the good intentions in the world won't help me memorize Scripture, because I am borderline blind. Like a bat. Or a mole. I'll try again tomorrow.

DAY 2: THE SERMON ON THE MOUNT

For simplicity's sake, I'm going to draw from the same linear passage of Scripture. Of all the chunks of the Bible I wish I had at my fingertips, the Sermon on the Mount from Matthew 5 is near the top of the list. Jesus' most lengthy teaching, centered on love of God and neighbor, is something I'd love to devote more time to learning. So today it begins.

When Jesus saw the crowds, he went up on a mountainside and sat down. His disciples came to him, and he began to teach them.

He said: "Blessed are the poor in spirit, for theirs is the kingdom of heaven."

DAY 3: EAT THIS BOOK

I memorized a ton of Scripture as a kid. My church was big on Bible memorization, and I'm grateful. But after high school, my memorization took a huge nosedive. I turned to English literature and then to theology textbooks and listening to too much Dashboard Confessional.

The goal this month isn't memorization, but I'm finding that the verses I shower with in the morning are already becoming part of me. If I read them while I shower, I have them with me for a moment, but if I work a bit to remember them, to store them away with all those childhood passages, I have them forever.

DAY 4: PAUSING FOR REFLECTION

It's so easy to speed through Scripture without stopping to think about what the words really mean, chewing on them and pondering them and letting them do their good work. As I start to spend these few precious moments with a verse or two from Scripture, it's like really listening to the lyrics of a song for the first time, discovering there's much more to them than first met your ear.

The Beatitudes are familiar. *Blessed are the poor in spirit. Blessed are those who mourn. Blessed are those who hunger and thirst for what is right.* But what do they *mean?* The word for *blessed* in Greek—the original language of the New Testament—can also be translated as "happy," which makes the passages more confusing still. *Happy* are those who grieve? *Happy* are the poor? Since when? In whose opinion?

In seasons of mourning, I certainly haven't *felt* happy. Grief is weighty, exhausting. It can be unbearably, achingly sorrowful. *Happy are those who mourn* is a little like saying *happy are the sad.* So perhaps this Scripture is getting at a deeper truth. One more profound than a fleeting feeling, a momentary emotion. The verses each have a second half: the explanation for the blessing, the happiness. The poor in spirit are blessed *because* the kingdom of heaven is theirs. Those who mourn are happy *because* they will be comforted. Those who hunger and thirst for righteousness will not hunger and thirst forever—they will one day be filled.

Each verse leaves the agency implicit. Who comforts? Who fills? Who ushers in this new reality? Jesus does. Blessed, happy, grieving, poor. The paradox of the kingdom.

DAY 5: MORNINGS ARE NOT MY THING

Today's Scripture was Matthew 5:5. I got out my marker and my Bible and proceeded to write Matthew 5:4 on the shower wall, right next to Matthew 5:4 from yesterday, because the preschooler had a nightmare at 2 a.m., the toddler woke up at 5:15 a.m., Daryl is out of town at a conference all week, and saying I'm tired doesn't even begin to describe it.

Apparently God wanted me to spend extra time with the verse about those who mourn being comforted. And perhaps the ache of exhaustion resounding in my body that cries out for respite, for rest, is in a way its own type of mourning.

DAY 6: THE BEATITUDES ARE WEIRD

Certain passages of Scripture make no earthly sense on paper. I'm struggling with the Beatitudes more than I expected. They're familiar, they're poetic, and they're also totally bonkers. Blessed are those who mourn? (Yes, I'm still stuck on this one.) In what parallel universe?

Douglas Hare connects it to Isaiah 61:1–4, which links mourning to poverty and injustice. Luke's version says "Blessed are you that weep now, for you shall laugh."[37] Hare describes Jesus' immediate context as "reasonably prosperous" but unequal.

He writes, "As in our own age, it was easy for the affluent to be unconcerned about the agony of the poor. There were many, nonetheless, who mourned the injustice of a system rigged in favor of the rich and powerful.... As we mourn our shared sinfulness, we receive assurance that our struggle for justice is not futile."[38] Scripture's interplay between mourning what is wrong and holding on to hope that God will make things right is a difficult and beautiful balancing act. So often I fall off the cliff on one side or the other—despair at everything that is wrong, or pie-in-the-sky belief that things will be just fine and dandy if we simply wait them out. Instead, Scripture gives permission to lament, while also calling us to hope.

Blessed are those who mourn.

DAY 7: A BOOK OF ITS OWN

Reading Scripture is so very different than reading anything else. I drink in novels—often two or three concurrently. Daryl and I trace the kids' interests at the library, picking up books on sharks or history or cooking, depending on what our boys want to learn. (My advice? Soft-pedal the nutrition books. Now I have a tiny five-year-old following me around the kitchen lecturing about how frosting is "a red light food. That means it's *bad*, Mommy. And you *really* shouldn't eat it from the can with a spoon like that.")

Yet with Scripture, reading is not primarily entertainment or information-gathering or even discovering a new perspective. It is all of these things, but not *only* these things. To read Scripture is to invite God into our minds, our hearts, and our lives, asking the Holy Spirit to do the hard and wonderful work of the gospel in us. As Benedictine Macrina Wiederkehr puts it, "We do not always realize what a radical suggestion it is for us to read to be formed and transformed rather than to gather information."[39] It's counterintuitive, but oh, so good.

Reading Scripture is an exercise in open heart surgery—far from a painless process. I don't do vulnerability easily or well. I don't think many of us do. Yet to read Scripture is to open ourselves up to the creative handiwork of God convicting, challenging, encouraging, and inviting us to give up that we may gain all. It's impossible to read Scripture thoughtfully and remain the same for long.

DAY 8: SWEETLY INCOMPETENT

Blessed are the pure in heart, for they will see God. This verse reminds me of my kids. The naiveté of a child—so trusting, so tender. I remember a pastor once saying that Jesus says we should become like a little child not because children are innocent but because they are unencumbered by self-awareness. I chuckled, but the sentiment stuck with me. I'm far too self-aware for my own good, if I'm honest.

Lisa Sharon Harper writes that we need to see ourselves and our neighbors and all of humanity as God does—"beloved dust."[40] Created as we are from the dirt, there is great freedom in accepting our place before God. We are adored not because we are good or pure or innocent or holy. We are none of these things. We are adored because God created us and loves us enough to breathe life into us again and again, to make us and remake us in his image.

To be pure in heart is not to be naturally undefiled. *Lead me not into temptation*, the Lord's Prayer says; and then we may add, tongue-in-cheek, *I can find the way myself.* To be pure in heart is to long for what is right, even as we struggle to do it. To seek after what is true, even when the lead boots of systemic and corporate and generational and personal sin pull us down.

Put another way: if we are looking for God, we will find him.

DAY 9: OWWWWWWW

There's a scene in the classic Bill Murray film *What about Bob?* when Bob (played by Murray) meets with his therapist, who tells him some harsh truths.

"So what you're saying is, even though you are an almost paralyzed, multi-phobic personality that is in a constant state of panic, your wife did not leave you, you left her because she liked Neil Diamond."

"Now you're saying that maybe I didn't leave her because she likes Neil Diamond, but maybe she left me?" Bob asks.

"Yes."

Bob then begins clutching his chest in pain.

"Owwwwwww," he says. "Ow! Ow! Ow!" He stops suddenly and looks his therapist straight in the eye. "Dr. Marvin," he says, finally, his eyes widening in amazement, "you can help me."[41]

It's often the sharp edge of truth, the one that cuts right to our core, that allows a breakthrough to take place.

Lincoln has been testing his boundaries a bit this week. He's a smart kid, and sometimes that big brain of his tempts him to question authority, to talk back, to wear his parents out with snark. Over the past three days, he and I have been locked in a battle where he comes back at me with sarcasm and eye rolls after practically every single thing I say. On the first day I handled it pretty well. By the second day my patience was wearing thin. By the third day, I'd *had* it.

"Sit there on the couch," I said, pointing. "Time-out."

"Until when?" he asked.

"Until I say so, and if you talk back while you're in time-out, no dessert."

"But I—"

"Okay then, no dessert." Cue the tears. No one tells you that at some point your kids will grow smarter than you, and disciplining them will get reaaaaaally tricky. Definitely no one tells you that this might happen by the time they're five.

There was more wailing at the dinner table and more consequences at bedtime. I became the mom in *I Love You Forever* who feels like she lives in a zoo. Wilson watched all of this with wide eyes, alternately patting his crying brother's shoulder and looking at me like, "Seriously, Mom?" By the third time Lincoln came out of his room long past his bedtime to argue with us about why his leg was just *way* too itchy for sleep, I wordlessly scooped him up and deposited him back in his bed.

"But Mom—" he called after me.

"BED," I said, shutting the door not-so-gently behind me as I left.

Brushing my teeth later that night, I leaned into the shower to close the sliding glass door and glanced at the Scripture wall.

Blessed are the peacemakers, for they will be called children of God.

Ouch. Ow, ow, ow, owwwwwww.

The thing is, I have no idea how to do this in my own house. A little help, Jesus?

DAY 10: ACCEPTING THE INVITATION

My dad knows that if he leaves me a voicemail with one particular phrase on it, I'm sure to return his call. That phrase? "You don't have to call me back." There's something about that release of obligation and expectation which frees me to treat his call as kindness and invitation rather than guilt or imperative.

As a kid, I often wondered why God doesn't just force us to be good, to love him, to follow him. He invites, but he never arm-twists. Forced love is no love at all. It's in this invitation that the life-giving power of the gospel truly begins to take hold.

"Thou *mayest*," the wise, patient Lee says in John Steinbeck's *East of Eden*.[42] The door is left open and it's up to us to walk through it.

This is how we grow in any area of life. No one becomes a professional athlete by being cajoled into lifting weights. No concert pianist can wring aching beauty from Debussy and Chopin because a teacher or a parent threatened her into practicing her skills. In every instance of devotion, there was a choice, a love, a desire to follow a path of discipline because of the joy, the reward, the goal. We all choose—this or that, how much, how far, how serious, how earnest. And each choice shapes us for deeper ones down the line. If I want to be a person more in tune with the challenging, haunting, uplifting truths in Scripture, I must choose to study today here and now. Not because I have to, but because this is who I want to be.

DAY 13: UNDER-SEASONED

We watch a lot of *Top Chef*, Daryl and I. There's something so fantastically, delightfully petty about a food critic wrinkling his nose and proclaiming with utter disdain, "Well, the fish was perfectly cooked but it was a little... *under-seasoned*," as if the chef in question is guilty not of missing a pinch of salt but of forgetting to wear pants to the opera. To under-season anything is a cardinal sin on cooking shows; commit it once, and you'll be sent to pack your knives.

I'm not much of a foodie, unless you count having tried every existing variety of Sour Patch Kids (word of advice: avoid the tropical ones), but those who are know that seasoning is everything. Back in Jesus' day, seasoning wasn't just nice for the palate; it was potentially life-saving. Think about it—no refrigeration in a hot, arid climate? Yikes. Salt acted as a preservative, taking food that would spoil in hours and extending its edibility by days or even weeks.

You are the salt of the earth, Jesus says to the crowd. Not *I am*, but *you are*. Preserve these truths. Bring out their flavor. Wake up the taste buds of the world, and then satisfy them with rich food. *Don't lose your saltiness.*

DAY 14: NEVER UNDERESTIMATE CONVENIENCE

I ran a (very slow) marathon in college, back when I had loads of free time and an unlimited pass to a dining hall's mountainous carbohydrates. In my thirties, I wanted to run another one, but I had zero motivation. I'd talk about it and download marathon training plans and look out the window at a perfect Saturday afternoon, and then I'd sigh and pick up a book or flip on the TV.

My friend Jinelle won a silver medal in Olympic women's ice hockey a handful of years ago. I asked her once where she got the determination. From the time we were kids, she spent her summers in the weight room while the rest of us tanned at the lake.

"I mean, some days don't you feel like *not* working out?" I asked.

"I don't allow it to be a choice," she said. "Training is just what I do." I pondered this. How could I get back to running without having to drum up the impulse to do it on my own? Finally, it hit me: what if, four or five days a week, I laced up my running shoes and left the house? Once I did that, I could choose to do whatever I wanted—I could run, but I could also pick dandelions or go sit at the park or meander down to the neighborhood coffee shop and fill myself with muffins. All I had to do was put on my shoes and step outside.

An amazing thing began to happen. Suddenly, I ran. Regularly. Willingly. Because it wasn't forced upon me, but also because once I was set up to do it, more often than not it was easiest just to go for the run. "I've already gotten this far," I'd say to myself. "Might as well exercise, too."

I wish I could say I ran another 26.2 miles after that, but I didn't. I did finish a half marathon, though, and then a solid 10k with a personal best time. I began looking forward to evenings with the setting sun and my beat-up sneakers, or early mornings with the dew fading and the town below my hilltop trail just starting to wake. Jesus showed up a lot, meeting me in the morning and evening quiet, interrupted by only my pounding footfalls and the occasional barking dog.

So much of practicing spiritual things is setting the stage beforehand, making it easier to do them than not. Writing verses in the shower where I'm sure to see them is such a tiny thing, but even that small, simple taste of God's goodness makes me hungry for more.

DAY 17: IN ITS FULLNESS

The shower was already steamed up when I got in it today. Daryl showered first, and a thick mist still hung in the air. He loves a hot shower. He tends toward the ascetic side, toward juice cleanses and meat-free months and pushing his body to the limit, so luxuriating in this daily, scalding ritual is one of his few real indulgences. Whenever he's out of sorts, I nudge him toward the shower. It always seems to help.

Through the steam I read Jesus' words: *Do not think that I have come to abolish the Law or the Prophets; I have not come to abolish them but to fulfill them.* To those worried that he was ushering in an entirely new system, promoting a different God, Jesus says no. I *am* the fulfillment. I am what you've been waiting for, the gospel made known, the Word made flesh, here, standing before you today.

What does it mean for the Law and the Prophets to be fulfilled? What would it mean for *you* to be fulfilled? For me? At the births of both of our sons, I remember holding each of them in my arms for the very first time and looking into their eyes. For all of the sacrifices and discomforts of pregnancy and birth—heartburn and backaches and stretch marks and contractions and tearing—I didn't yet know this little person. Each of my sons spent nine months listening to my heart beat, eating what I ate, being sustained by my breath; but they were almost complete mysteries to me. Then, when I finally saw their tiny faces—fulfillment. So *this* is my baby. *This* is my son.

What would it have felt like to pray and hope for the Messiah, the Coming One, the Promised Savior, and to hear Jesus say those words? Some would certainly have scoffed. *Messiah? I don't think so. I thought he'd be taller.* Others would ponder the implications of such a statement. If it really *was* true, then what did it mean for them, for their families, for their community, for the world? Still others—a handful at first, then dozens, then hundreds—believed what Jesus said. There he was: the fulfillment.

DAY 20: FEAR AND TREMBLING

I worry about being a mother. Beyond the usual worries—germs, manners, this school or that one—I worry that the weight of such a responsibility will crush me. These tiny humans with their great big souls live in my house, eat at my table, and are entrusted to my care. It feels practically impossible to live up to this importance—I *will* do and say the wrong thing; I *will* and *do* lose my patience; I *will* and *do* discipline when I should show mercy, and then let the kids walk all over me when what they need is a firm boundary to lean against. Jesus' words from Matthew 5 are searing into my soul this morning: *Therefore anyone who sets aside one of the least of these commands and teaches others accordingly will be called least in the kingdom of heaven, but whoever practices and teaches these commands will be called great in the kingdom of heaven.*

Parenthood is all about teaching. Sometimes we teach in words, but more often through our actions. I can tell Lincoln to speak kindly all I want, but when I mutter under my breath that the guy who just cut me off in traffic should go home until he learns how to operate heavy machinery, guess who is listening from the backseat? Lately he's developed this little sigh-and-eye-roll routine I know he's learned from me, because the last few times he stretched his normal twenty-minute bedtime routine to over an hour, that's how I responded.

The passage continues: *For I tell you that unless your righteousness surpasses that of the Pharisees and the teachers of the law, you will certainly not enter the kingdom of heaven.* It can be hard to catch (humor doesn't always translate well across languages and centuries and cultures), but Jesus is being ironic here. The Pharisees and teachers of the law were known far and wide for their attention to detail when it came to righteousness. "You give a tenth of all your spices," Jesus says later, pointing out the precision with which they followed the law. Yet by and large, these same groups were known for lacking compassion: "But you have neglected the more important matters of the law—justice, mercy and faithfulness."[43] Practice the latter, Jesus says, without neglecting the former. It isn't that the law isn't important; it's that the heart of the law matters, too. It isn't enough to do all the right outward things while being obstinate, hate-filled, and merciless.

The responsibility is a serious one—weighty and significant. Yet its core call is to teach the faith: in many ways the greatest and most vital task of parenthood. Today getting both kids dressed and fed feels like a victory. Sometimes it feels like the gospel asks a little too much of us. Perhaps that's the point. When we reach our end, we are much more likely to run to Jesus.

DAY 24: BLESSED ARE THE PEACE-FAKERS

Therefore, if you are offering your gift at the altar and there remember that your brother or sister has something against you, leave your gift there in front of the altar. First go and be reconciled to them; then come and offer your gift.

There Jesus goes again, paying attention to the heart of the matter rather than its outward appearance. Kinda like it's his thing.

DAY 28: MARINATING

I'm a fast cook. Dinner in twenty minutes, as many ingredients as possible in one pot or pan; salt, sauté, stir, serve. I'm also not what most people would consider a *good* cook. I'm not self-conscious about it; it just is. We eat lots of quesadillas. I count chicken nuggets as viable entrees. We do okay by nutrition—everyone has a vegetable on their plate, we try to go easy on the sugar—but gourmands, we are not. You simply can't cook incredible food in twenty minutes, except on *Top Chef.* Truly good food takes time. It takes thought and preparation and focus and love.

Whenever we visit my parents in Wisconsin, they cook steak. Red meat is one of Daryl's love languages—when he's not on one of his weird cleanses—and for most of our married life we've been in graduate school, relating on an intimate level to Kate Bowler's experience: "I was in school for a decade," she wrote, "and we were almost comically poor. Not poor like sweet church mice. Poor like people who worried we would get scurvy because we couldn't afford to buy oranges."[44] We don't buy our own steak. Ever. So my parents welcome us with these ridiculously good, melt-in-your-mouth filets. And Lincoln always asks, with wonder in his eyes, "Why don't we eat this *all the time*?"

So one day I decided to surprise Daryl by cooking steak at home. I went to the store, bought a flat package from the meat fridge labeled STEAK, and came home and seared it up in a pan (I'm all for equal rights for women, just don't make me learn how to work a charcoal grill), then finished it in the oven, oh-so-proud to present it to my family. I had made *steak*. Me, mighty CaveWoman™ hunter and provider.

We all sat down to dinner, flowers on the table, a fresh salad and rolls and baked potatoes at the ready, even though I knew the boys would ignore them because *meat*, and we dug in. Linc took a few bites and then looked up at me quizzically.

"Can I have some more bread?" he asked. Daryl picked at his food, carving off chunks of fat, poking and prodding.

I took my first bite. It wasn't steak; it was rubber.

"Did you marinate this in anything?" Daryl asked.

"Marinate?" I responded. I'd only decided to make a steak dinner a couple of hours earlier. Marinating is not the friend of the last-minute cook. A day or two later, I called my parents to learn their steak secrets.

"They're marinated in papaya juice," my dad said. "That's what makes them tender." Huh. Turns out you can't just heat up pricey meat and expect things to go well. Tough fibers take time to break down. Marinating is key.

So it is with the nourishment found in Scripture. We can survive on just a little bit—a bite here, a bite there, all eaten on the run, all purchased from the drive-thru. But Scripture is meant to be savored, to be soaked in. The beauty of a marinade is that it does its work while we go about our days. This is often true of Scripture, too. As Eugene Peterson puts it, spiritual reading is "reading that enters our souls as food enters our stomachs, spreads through our blood, and becomes holiness and love and wisdom."[45] When we immerse ourselves in the Word of God, it will work on us continually, challenging areas of sin, encouraging areas of growth, smoothing salve over our wounds, slowly but surely making us holy.

I've been continually amazed at how the Scriptures from the morning continued to show up throughout the day. It's as if God mapped out the whole picture, from the early moments in the shower until the late hour when my head hit the pillow. This month's experiment has taught me a great deal about the reward of learning Scripture, but even more about the work of God in and through these ancient words.

DAY 30: THE GIFT OF EASE

The biggest win this month has been having Scriptures so readily available. Distractions abound in the seasons of parenthood, and before this month I found myself in a consistent shame cycle about how easily I'd get turned from the pages of Scripture to another pressing task. As Hudson Taylor once put it, "Satan will always find you something to do when you ought to be occupied about [reading Scripture], even if it is only arranging a window blind."[46] It's much harder to be distracted in the shower, even if I only get a few moments in there to myself.

This month's exercise is going in the permanent catechesis toolbox at our house. I'd better order some more dry erase markers.

JOIN THE JOURNEY

Choose some Scripture that you'd like to meditate on during your showers. I found it helpful to choose a Scripture passage that had about twenty-five verses, knowing that I would likely miss a few days (five months into this experiment in spiritual practices, and I've become a realist!). Write them on the shower wall, or—if your shower isn't writeable—you may want to write them on index cards and slip them into a Ziploc bag. Suction cup hooks work well in most showers, or you can hang the bag from the showerhead itself.

Then all that's left is to let God work that Scripture into your mind while you wash off the cares of the day. I think you'll be surprised at how often the verse or two you showered with crops up unexpectedly to encourage or challenge you, and how soon the Scriptures start to become part of you.

Some Scriptures that you may want to use for this experiment:

> Psalm 89
> Isaiah 55
> Matthew 5:1–24
> Matthew 6:7–34
> Revelation 22

CHAPTER 7

FASTING FROM FACEBOOK

Giving Up to Gain

Fasting cleanses the soul.... Enter again into yourself.
—St. Augustine

A year or so ago, we traveled out of town for a couple nights as a family, all jammed into a single bedroom at a resort. Linc slept on a mattress on the floor, and little Wilson dozed in a portable crib. When the four of us woke the following morning, both boys wanted to snuggle. It was one of those greeting-card-perfect moments—everyone smiling and relaxed, warm from sleep, the boys with bedhead and rosy cheeks, my head nestled on Daryl's shoulder. But instead of drinking in the sleepy pajama-clad kids and the tender embrace of my husband, I rolled over, picked up my phone, and surfed the internet, completely ignoring a beautiful, perhaps once-in-a-lifetime moment.

In the hours that followed, the sin of my distraction burned my heart. Will I remember what so-and-so posted on social media when I'm old and gray? No, but I might have remembered that early morning, cuddling on the bed with my boys. Now I just remember *missing* it. And for what? The ease of not having to engage with actual humans? The quick rush of being spoon-fed sugar instead of feasting on the rich meal of love right in front of me? The enslaving addiction to any screen within viewing distance?

This incident took place over a year ago, yet I still think about it. I've changed my social media habits since, pared down my phone so that my screen is grayscale and I can't get online easily. But the question remains: Why do I continually choose distraction over engagement, even when the distraction is not something I actually *want*? Am I lazy? So mired in easy sin that I can't climb out? Or is there something deeper—and more troubling—at work?

What it comes down to, I think, is that engaging with technology is nearly always the easiest thing. It provides instant gratification; it's always available; it offers uncomplicated interaction at our beck and call, literally at our fingertips. Unlike a real-life human being, it requires nothing of us in return.

Beyond that, technology doesn't just tempt us to zone out from the physical and communal and familial worlds right in front of us; over time and with repeated use, it changes us, making it ever more difficult to choose the real over the ephemeral. Notes Marc Prensky, "Based on the latest research in neurobiology, there is no longer any question that stimulation of various kinds actually changes brain structures."[47] My guess is that you've felt this yourself. Journalist Nicholas Carr writes:

> Over the past few years I've had an uncomfortable sense that someone, or something, has been tinkering with my brain, remapping the neural circuitry, reprogramming the memory.

My mind isn't going—so far as I can tell—but it's changing. I'm not thinking the way I used to think....Once I was a scuba diver in the sea of words. Now I zip along the surface like a guy on a Jet Ski.[48]

Instead of investing in the deep, real things of life—the slow things that take time and effort and patience and perseverance— the digital world has begun to train us for impatience, impermanence, and instant gratification. It isn't that we lack willpower— though willpower is a piece of the equation—it's that we are being conditioned, and allowing ourselves to be conditioned, to a different way of life that has come on the scene so quickly and changes and updates itself so often that psychologists, psychiatrists, and pastors alike are reeling to try to respond to it in a timely way.

FASTING

GIVING UP, FOR A SET AMOUNT OF TIME, SOMETHING YOU REGULARLY CONSUME IN ORDER TO DEVOTE THAT TIME TO PRAYER.

BEING ATTENTIVE TO WHAT HAPPENS WITHIN YOU WHEN HUNGERS CREATED BY YOUR FAST ARISE.

Digital technology is too tempting for me, and I'm guessing it is for you, too. A level of overdependence, compulsion, or even addiction to this sphere is an all-too-common problem. I'm not judging—many parents (myself included) often work remotely, and that phone is the device that allows them to be with their kids rather than locked in an office all day. The magic of the online universe can connect us with far-flung relatives and provide community beyond what is present to us in our everyday circumstances. More personally, this book would simply not exist without my online writing cohorts. Yet the temptation to give technology more than its due is a real and ever-present one, and one to which we too often acquiesce.

Every once in a while, Lincoln will put his hand over my phone and say, "Look at *me*, Mommy." He's almost six years old. I will not get these years back. Maybe the only way out is to jettison the cell phone altogether. In his *Letters from the Desert*, Carlo Carretto writes, "Jesus…became flesh, lived among people, and he embodied the Gospel message in its entirety. He began to act. He lived his message before he *spoke* of it. He preached it by his life before explaining it in words."[49] My telling Linc he's important to me means nothing if I'm always sucked into my phone. He isn't likely to tell me his fears and worries when he's a teenager if I haven't engaged with them when he's five.

In *Uncluttered* I wrote about some of the radical changes Daryl and I made in our digital lives to help untangle us from the bondage of constant connectedness. Some people can probably have a fully loaded smartphone and still be engaged in real life more than in the virtual space. I can't. There is always something new to look at or look up or click into, and I've come to realize that I rarely have the types of interactions with my kids I want when I have a phone or computer within arm's reach. Willpower is too weak to rely upon when the exhaustion of the day presses in, never mind trying to hold fast to Luddite principles when thousands of engineers are working behind the screen to get me to click just *one more link*.

This knowledge that it isn't simply me versus the screen is actually quite illuminating. "'You could say that it's my responsibility' to exert self-control when it comes to digital usage," explains Tristan Harris, once a Design Ethicist at Google and now founder and executive director of the Center for Humane Technology, "but that's not acknowledging that there's a thousand people on the other side of the screen whose job is to break down whatever responsibility I can maintain."[50] If you, like me, struggle with the cycle of digital compulsion and shame (check the email, check the social media sites, realize you've ignored your kids, feel like The Worst Mom Ev-ah, repeat, repeat, repeat), this is good news, in a way. It isn't simply that human beings are weak-willed (though we can be, and the more we acquiesce to the easiest things rather than the best things, the harder our will is to shape in the ways we—and God—desire); it's also that the digital game is far more insidious and invasive and far-reaching than a single person's battle for self-control.

But now for the good news—I'd even call it Good News—which is, we don't have to acquiesce to a world of pings and clicks and dings. There is another way, a far better one. God has provided an empowering, grace-filled way for us to begin throwing off that which threatens to enslave us. We *can* recover our God-given freedom. I knew I needed to do something radical, something that didn't rely solely on my own energy and ability to make good digital decisions every moment of every day. Then I realized: Lent started in three days.

It was time to fast.

You may or may not be into Lent; not all Christians follow liturgical practices, and of those who do, not all participate in Lenten fasting over the forty days that precede the celebration of Easter. But whether you engage the season of Lent or not, Jesus is pretty serious about fasting. He talks about it in Scripture as a *when* practice, not an *if.*[51]

Fasting from food is an important spiritual practice, but it won't work for all of us all the time. For example, I've basically spent the better part of a decade carrying a pregnancy or nursing a baby, so fasting from food has been tricky. Babies gotta *eat*. My good friend Amanda suffered from a serious eating disorder in high school, so fasting from food is off the table for her as well. If you're diabetic or have certain other health conditions, food fasts can create a real medical risk.

Still, Jesus' call to fast is clear. The good news is that we don't have to abstain from *food* in order to fast. There is scriptural precedent for giving up other things. In her book *Fasting: Spiritual Freedom Beyond Our Appetites*, Lynne Baab devotes a chapter to other types of fasting, citing Paul's words in 1 Corinthians 7:5:

> Paul does say…that a couple can choose to refrain from sexual intimacy by mutual agreement 'for a set time, to devote yourselves to prayer.' Paul doesn't use the word *fast*, but this is a pattern that can inform our engagement in fasting from things other than food. [52]

Elsewhere in Scripture we find Moses instructing the Israelites to consecrate themselves (make themselves holy) by fasting from sexual intercourse for three days. [53] We read that Daniel gave up using body oils and lotions (both commonly used for hygiene rituals) for three weeks, in addition to fasting from certain foods. [54]

While abstaining from food is by far the most common type of biblical fasting, and something every Christian should participate in at some point if physically possible, at times other types of fasts may be not only the most practical but the most spiritually beneficial. I often fast by giving up other things: soda (a real sacrifice back when Dr. Pepper and I used to hang out every day), wearing colors (more on that in *Uncluttered*), and listening to the radio in the car (I ♥ NPR), just to name a few.

Fasting is a very straightforward spiritual discipline. Instead of taking on a new practice, we simply stop doing something.

Oftentimes it's most helpful to choose to abstain from a particular habit that has taken too large a place in our lives. As Lynne Baab notes,

> Sometimes we notice that aspects of our daily lives have become too important. In the past they may have been healthy and life-giving…but now for some reason they have grabbed ahold of us. They have assumed a place out of proportion to their true meaning and value. So we set them aside for a season to pray.[55]

I needed this more than I can say.

I feel the grip of social media on my attentions; it is not a loving master. It's also infiltrating my life in ways I never wanted. I'm more than ready to shed it for a season. For the next forty days, I'll be fasting from it. I'm not on Instagram at all anymore (I have an account, but couldn't tell you the last time I checked it); Facebook and Twitter are my particular brand of addiction. Today I'm signing off.

Pray for me, friends.

DAY 1: ASH WEDNESDAY

It's the afternoon of Ash Wednesday—the very first day in Lent—and I've already gone to my computer to check Twitter nine times. I haven't actually *checked* it, but I've gone there, my fingers poised over the keys before I realized what I'm doing. My digital habits? Apparently they're like a reflex.

Maybe Facebook and Twitter aren't your particular addictions, but I'm willing to bet there's at least one digital place where you spend more time than you'd like. Maybe it's a news app, a digital game, or a website you mindlessly scroll. Maybe you're Instagramobsessed, or you habitually check your work email in the middle of the night. Even my grandmother struggles to power down her tablet's puzzle app. Technological tentacles are no respecters of age or position.

So anyway, it's been half a day, and I've spent much of it unintentionally *almost* signing on to social media. I never knew Pavlov's dog and I had so much in common.

"This is terrible," I texted Daryl. "I already miss Twitter. I miss Facebook. What am I supposed to do with all the time I used to spend on social media?"

"Pray," he responded. "Read your Bible. Play with the kids." Daryl's not great at recognizing a rhetorical question. Cue all the eye rolls from me, because social media is fun, and those other things he mentioned often seem, well, *less so.*

Right, I said. *That's what I should do.* What I *did* do was stare at my email inbox waiting for something, anything, interesting to happen. Nothing did.

Sigh. It was going to be a long Lent.

DAY 1: UPDATE

A teenager shot up his former high school in Parkland, Florida this afternoon. Seventeen people died, mostly kids. Lord, have mercy.

Normally I'd process this tragedy with a small army of the armchair theologians (and a handful of actual ones) on Twitter and hundreds of acquaintances on Facebook. I imagine people are posting the same familiar threads and articles and memes about violence in America and gun control, reaming out politicians who offer #thoughtsandprayers instead of concrete action. Others are crying the opposite—that guns don't kill people, people kill people. Not that these discussions aren't worth having—we certainly must have them—but social media gets particularly nasty and reductive in times of tribulation. It's a relief not to witness the secondary carnage, to process the tragedy with Daryl and my coworkers and my church instead.

This is how we used to take in the news, isn't it? I was only weeks into my freshman year at Wheaton College, a Christian liberal arts school outside Chicago, on September 11, 2001. My professor was preparing to show our class a short video. When he turned on the television to put in the VHS tape (yes, I'm that old), we saw the first plane hit the towers. "What a horrible accident," he said. We paused and prayed, and he continued the class. By the end of hour, the second plane struck, and everyone began to realize it wasn't an accident. Far from home for the first time, I walked out into the autumn morning and followed a stream of students to the only place we knew to go: the chapel.

Wheaton requires its students to attend chapel on Mondays, Wednesdays, and Fridays, but this was a Tuesday. There was no scheduled chapel service. Still, nearly two thousand of us crowded into the wide brick building at the center of campus. The school's chaplain led us in prayer. We knelt together in the seats, in the aisles. Those with friends or relatives in New York City shook and wept. Fear and confusion, anger and dread: we brought them all into the house of God, sharing them with one another, pouring them out beneath the cross.

There was no social media back then, not really. Instead, we had Jesus. Each other. Professors and a student body president and a handful of chaplains. We grieved together. We began to make sense of what had happened together, in person, in academic hallways and dorm room lounges and college cafés.

A few of my new friends and I drove home the following weekend, up to my parents' place in Wisconsin. These eighteen- and nineteen-year-old kids were from California and New

Hampshire and New York and Washington, their homes too far away to reach in a weekend's drive, but we each longed to be in a place that felt calm and safe and far, far away from speeding planes and big cities. We hiked through the autumn woods and ate my dad's homemade chocolate chip cookies, letting my mom pamper us with meals and my sisters pester us by making up their own rules to *Clue*. We went to church Sunday morning and prayed for our country; for those who had lost loved ones; for peace; for the world. It was all so slow and rich and personal: the speed of our lament, of our prayers, of our processing.

Today I prayed for Parkland without a thousand screaming voices analyzing it for me. On CNN I saw a photo of a crying mother, her forehead marked with the ashen cross of the start of Lent, and I knelt. Instead of reading what others thought, I sat with Jesus and asked for mercy. Instead of being overwhelmed by a flood of different calls to action, I prayed about what God would have *me* do.

DAY 2: IT MIGHT NOT BE HEROIN, BUT IT'S AWFULLY ADDICTING

The withdrawal feelings? They are *serious*. I'm now constantly questioning my reality. If I have a snarky comment and don't post it to Twitter, do I even exist? I'm not sure. Catherine Marshall once wrote of a fast, "For the first half of the day, I simply felt a void, almost as if I had been wiped out as a person."[56] She gets me.

Fasting from social media has also hiked up my anxiety. What if someone I know dies, and I don't even find out about it because Facebook is usually where I get all of my interpersonal news? I'd like to think someone would call me, but people don't call anymore. They text. Or they send Facebook messages, including some of the oldest ladies at my church, who are far more tech savvy than they tend to let on.

I'm not sure who I am without the constant connectedness of social media. That, my friends, is a problem, and one I'm glad I have these next days to ponder.

DAY 3: TO THE NORTH

Our church's high school youth group holds its annual ski trip in Utah this weekend. Their retreat speaker dropped out at the last minute, so I got drafted. Though, to be honest, four days in the snowy mountains in a private condo without my kids sounds more like a vacation than any sort of work. I get to ski, too. If it weren't for the talks I needed to write for an age group I don't typically speak to in less than three days, I'd feel almost guilty about getting to have so much fun while Daryl keeps the small people alive back home.

The only part I was dreading—riding the bus for ten hours with forty caffeinated teenagers (which sounded like some sort of punishment)—made for a surprisingly good time. This particular bus full of Generation Z was made up of inquisitive, bright, hilarious teenagers. Besides the one who somehow fell asleep in the overhead luggage compartment ("He does this every year," one of his friends told me), they were also remarkably mellow and well behaved. I didn't even see the ubiquitous smartphones in their hands as often as I'd thought I might. Instead, they were talking. Playing cards. Hopping back and forth between clusters of girls and clusters of guys. Eating an obscene amount of Doritos.

Without social media as my pacifier, by southern Nevada I'd already worked on the talks for a couple of hours, fielded a handful of theological questions from a particularly thoughtful teenager, and made it halfway through a novel. A few miles before we stopped for dinner, I actually saw a tumbleweed.

Then, of course, my desire to send a GIF of a tumbleweed to Daryl kicked in...Change is hard, friends. Change is hard.

DAY 5: REDEEMING TIME, OR AT LEAST NOTICING IT

My days feel longer now. I gave away *so much time* to social media. All in five-minute chunks, of course, but add that up over the course of a day, and it was easily over an hour or more. (Let's be honest. It was more.)

If someone rang my doorbell and asked for an hour of my time every day for a very good cause, I'd tell them they were crazy. I don't *have* an extra hour a day. I'm busy! My days are jam-packed! Yet I realize now I was willingly and regularly giving up that hour—an hour I could use to do any number of better, more lasting, more important things—to Mark Zuckerberg and the Twittersphere.

It's humbling to realize there was something so major about my daily life that I failed to notice at all before this fast. How often have I—have any of us—said we simply don't have time for something when we've always had it; we've just frittered it away on the useless, the unmemorable, the complete time-waster? Like Esau in the book of Genesis, who sold his birthright for a mess of stew, how often do I unknowingly sell mine for a quick dopamine hit? The magnitude of the problem is serious and tragic. I'm sobered. I'm chastened. I'm determined to make some permanent changes.

What can I do with this newfound time? The time that's been mine all along?

DAY 7: TIME TO CHANGE MY EMAIL SETTINGS

I have twenty-nine new Twitter notifications!

Social media is so faithful in emailing to tell me that I am dangerously out of the loop. The algorithm doesn't send the content of the tweets, of course, but it constantly reminds me that I'm missing *allthethings*. Social media taps into that place in each of us that is fearful of being out of the loop. Time to reroute some emails to the spam folder.

DAY 9: FOMO. SERIOUS FOMO.

The daughter of dear friends of ours has cancer. She's five years old. It blows my mind and breaks my heart. But here's my current dilemma: They post updates about her in a private Facebook group. We pray for her and live close enough that we offer to help with meals or rides or babysitting, but now that I'm off social media, I have no earthly idea what's going on with her or with them.

Daryl logged on for me today to check. I hope that's not cheating. Also: she's doing really well. Praise Jesus.

DAY 12: QUIETER, SLOWER, HARDER, BETTER

"I'm lonelier than I expected," I told Daryl last night. We chatted over dinner: a rare date night out, holding hands over lemongrass pork with crispy shallots. "I didn't realize how the little comments and likes and shares online filled up almost all my need for social interaction. They weren't substantive connections with people, but they were often all I needed to feel socially attached."

"Worth exploring," he said, squeezing my hand. "You gonna finish those pickled veggies?"

DAY 17: INTROVERTS UNITE! ALONE AND IN SEPARATE HOUSES

I've always been an introvert. I used to be only borderline, but since going into ministry—much of which is very people-centric—I've become much more so. At the end of a day, I'm usually pretty talked out. I love meeting friends or congregants for lunch, but by dinner I've nearly always run out of words entirely.

During this fast, my social energy has begun to return. I'm looking for opportunities to get together with friends, waiting for the neighbor kids to come out to play, seeking out activities that I'd otherwise forego. Perhaps my introversion is not heightened by ministry alone, but by spending my people energy in fits and starts on the internet instead of in real life.

As this fast forces me to enter more fully and regularly into the physical realities of my life, I'm finding my appetites beginning to shift. God is so gracious that way—having created us for the real, the more we choose it, the easier and more satisfying it becomes to choose. Kind of like how we put peas on Lincoln's plate for a solid year and watched him throw them on the floor, mash them into his hair, and ignore them completely—until one day he took a tentative nibble, smiled, and said, "Hey! These are actually kinda good!"

DAY 20: BREAKING THE CHAINS

There's a significant difference between fasting from something inherently necessary—like food—and fasting from something optional. Unlike times I've abstained from food for an afternoon or a day, or even fasted from a particular food group like sweets for the entire season of Lent, giving up social media is making me crave it *less*, not more. The boredom has—for the most part—faded. I feel happy more frequently, and that happiness is, well, *happier.* One researcher discovered how true this was for teens as well. "There's not a single exception," she wrote. "All screen activities are linked to less happiness, and all nonscreen activities are linked to more happiness."[57]

I'm realizing how often I let the virtual words of others—sometimes friends, but more often only distant acquaintances—dictate my mood, my thoughts, what I percolate on during the day. Daryl and I have begun to have deeper conversations about issues—politics, education, mission—around the dinner table, listening to one another before we invite the clamor of outside opinions. I've found myself reading more news from a wider array of sources rather than taking in the sound bites from the loudest voices. Thinking critically is hard to do—I'd almost argue it *can't* be done—in 280 characters, or a flippant Facebook post composed in seconds. With less time online, I have more time to think deeply and read widely.

The longer this fast continues, the more rooted I feel to the real life right in front of me. Richard Foster writes, "Fasting helps us keep our balance in life. How easily we begin to allow nonessentials to take precedence in our lives. How quickly we crave things we do not need until we are enslaved by them."[58] Slavery is a strong word for addiction to superfluous things, but he isn't wrong. Scripture describes it in a similar way: "People are slaves to whatever has mastered them."[59] Whatever the yearnings are that steer our lives, if they are outside of the gospel imperative—love God, love neighbor—we must break their yoke of slavery. God gives us freedom; let us not unintentionally give it up to the infiltrations of the digital world.

Sometimes a fast can help; other times we may need to change certain habits, rework our schedules, install technological safeguards, see a professional counselor, or even attend a rehab program. There's no shame in getting help to get untangled. We *all* need it from time to time.

DAY 25: A DELIGHTFUL ODDITY

I sat next to one of Lincoln's former preschool teachers at a lunch yesterday. We got to chatting, and she mentioned an upcoming local event.

"It's on Facebook!" she said, pointing to my phone. "My phone's out of batteries, but if you pull it up, I'll show you."

"I'm not on Facebook right now," I told her. "I actually don't even have internet access on my phone." She pondered this for a moment, looking curiously at my iPhone—a device designed with getting online as one of its primary purposes.

"That's an interesting choice," she said. "I'm going to have to think about that."

DAY 33: REAL-LIFE FRIENDS

It's my friend Orva's birthday today, so she and two other girlfriends and I met up at the park to celebrate while letting our kids play together. Three out of the four of us, including Orva, aren't on social media at all right now. "It just wasn't helping," she once told me. When we need each other, we call or text. When we miss each other, we get together. When we want to share news, we do it personally. It's delightfully old-fashioned and oh-so-good.

It helps me to remember that the entire world *isn't* on social media: that another path is possible, and maybe even better than the most popular path. Perhaps it's preferable to cultivate intimate friendship with a few rather than halfhearted acquaintance-level niceties with hundreds.

DAY 40: A NECESSARY EVIL, OR A CLEAN BREAK?

This fast ends tomorrow. To be honest, I'm not at all excited about logging back on to social media. I'm actually a little terrified. I know I'm not good at halfhearted practices; I'm either all in or all out, logging in multiple times a day or completely turned off. Tuning out has been a gift; I've gained time, rediscovered friendships, thought more deeply and critically about important issues, and found greater stillness for my ping-ponging soul.

Yet social media has become something of a necessary evil, particularly within the spheres of writing and ministry, which is largely where I exist. Facebook is where I learn of ministry needs in my immediate community—from deaths to lost dogs. Twitter helps connect me with other writers, pastors, speakers, thinkers. There's the legitimate reality that I need social media to help publicize my books. Yet how many of these things are genuine needs, and how many are sugarcoated excuses to log back in to my favorite time-wasting hobby?

I'm struggling with how to log back on responsibly, how to not let it encroach upon my life and friendships and faith and—more than anything else—my *time*. If I can't simply sign off forever—the most courageous and also, in many ways, the *easiest* option to keep social media's disruptions at bay—I need to think long and hard about how I invite it back into my daily routine.

"Fasting is a good safeguard for the soul," St. Basil the Great once preached.[60] Perhaps therein lies the secret. Daryl and I already fast from electronics on our family Sabbath. Maybe extending that to a daily fast—8 p.m. to 8 a.m., and all mealtimes, or something like that—is the key. Andy Crouch writes of his family's digital practices in *The Tech-Wise Family*. Rather than jettison all technology, they adopt periodic fasts. One hour a day, one day a week, and one week a year, the whole family puts their electronics away and reconnects with what is right in front of them.[61] This may be a best practice for our family going forward, too. True fasting points us toward integrating the virtues it builds into every part of our lives, to deepening practices that make us more fully alive, more fully human, more fully in tune with the wild wind of the Holy Spirit.

Tomorrow I break my fast. It will be Easter morning, the glorious feast of the resurrection. The morning will usher in a new liturgical season with new opportunities to be faithful in my use of social media. I'm nervous. But perhaps facing this with a level of fear and trembling is not such a bad thing.

JOIN THE JOURNEY

Log off social media—*all* social media. If forty days seems too long, just start somewhere. A day. A week. If self-control isn't your thing (and seriously, no judgment, I'm eating coffee cake at 4:21 p.m. as I type this), ask someone you trust to change your passwords for you for a season. If you legitimately need it for your job (be ruthlessly honest—in many cases you can ask someone else to manage it, or else take a month-long breather without bankrupting the business), limit your use to only working hours.

Watch your time open up. Notice your awareness returning. Pay attention to what happens within and around you, to what God brings to the forefront in a season with fewer digital distractions. Consider never going back.

Some Scriptures to help guide you along the way:

Exodus 34:28
Joel 2:12–13
Matthew 6:16–18
Luke 4:2–4

CHAPTER 8

SUFFERING & STILLNESS
Because Sometimes All You Can Do Is Nothing

Let it come, as it will, and don't be afraid.
God does not leave us comfortless, so let evening come.
—Jane Kenyon

No one ever hopes to learn about suffering from experience. We might read about it, watch movies highlighting it, meet with friends going through it, work with those at greater risk for it, or visit a hospital or hospice and see it up close. But when the suffering is our own—when it is *personal*—it can be difficult to find meaning and hope. It can feel nearly impossible even to put one foot in front of the other.

In the middle of winter, watching our two kids play with Legos, their little angel-faces fixed in those half-smile, half-frowns kids get when they're concentrating fiercely, Daryl and I decided to open our family to the possibility of a third child. *It'll take months*, we thought. *Maybe even years.* I was thirty-five years old, for one thing, the age at which doctors and obstetricians put the fear of God into you because you are now *of Advanced Maternal Age*, which makes it sound like you should consider crypt-keeper over baby-raiser. On top of that, Daryl and I each faced solo travels that month, making it difficult to perform certain baby-making activities on the regular. Yet the Lord worked, as he sometimes does, very quickly, and before we knew it, we were both staring at a positive pregnancy test with our mouths hanging open.

"Well," said Daryl, "I didn't expect *that*."

"Oh *no*," I said, doing the math, "I'm going to be in my third trimester during the hottest time of the year." We felt happy, to be sure, but unlike the euphoria we experienced with our first two babies, we were also immediately shot through with a hard dose of realism. Carrying a child is not easy or without risk. Our youngest hadn't yet turned two years old, meaning we'd have two children under age three when this new one joined us. There were logistics to manage at the office with parental leave occurring during Advent—one of the busiest seasons of the church year. I'd be out of the pulpit on Christmas Eve; we wouldn't be able to travel to the Midwest to celebrate New Year's as we usually did.

But even beyond all that, a fledgling pregnancy opens up hope and heartache in a way few other things can. Most of us know people who have suffered miscarriages, struggled to make sense of difficult fetal diagnoses, or lost babies to stillbirth. A dear friend shared that she'd lost a baby just days earlier at ten-weeks gestation. The ultrasound photo looked perfect, the baby's profile already resembling dad, but there was no heartbeat. Opening a family to the possibility of new life is not without complication or risk.

"We have a ways to go," Daryl said, squeezing my hand. "One step at a time."

STILLNESS
REMAINING ROOTED BEFORE GOD;
PRACTICING QUIETNESS IN HIS PRESENCE.

After a couple of normal weeks, the difficulties began. Little One was healthy by all accounts and tests, but I quickly became a mess. With both our boys, I'd developed mild morning sickness— nausea and food aversions coupled with an unhelpfully strong sense of smell, which sometimes had me leaving restaurants before ordering and opening every window in the house even when temperatures plummeted. (Poor Daryl couldn't understand why he wasn't allowed to cook chicken anymore or why I'd loved root beer for three decades but suddenly couldn't tolerate even the mention of it. In sickness and in health, babe.) With the boys, my pregnancy malaise started consistently around seven weeks and lasted until eleven or twelve. It wasn't pleasant, but it was manageable. Besides the ginger ale and occasional naps, my first two pregnancies were pretty much business as usual for me.

But this time the nausea started at five weeks and ramped up about fifty-eight notches. From occasional queasiness, I moved rapidly to becoming borderline nonfunctional, unable to even enter our kitchen, to keep down any food but plain white rice, ice cold Gatorade, and an occasional handful of potato chips. (*Only* classic Ruffles. The one time Daryl brought home a bag of off-brand chips, I melted down into a puddle because *what*, was I supposed to try to *eat those*? LITTLE ONE HAD DEMANDS.) Unlike both of my previous pregnancies, this time I vomited. Regularly. Repeatedly. Constantly, and with little warning. I ducked out of meetings at work, sprinted to the bathroom in the middle of worship, and rarely kept anything down during the changing of each and every single diaper. I lost weight. I looked pale and gaunt. I couldn't stand the smell of dish soap, freshly cut grass, eucalyptus, my sons' shampoo, my husband's deodorant, our bedroom linens. The only thing that helped in the slightest was peppermint gum, and I began chewing packs of it a day, spitting it out only to throw up or to sleep. I preached on Good Friday with a wad of it stuffed into my cheek, causing every homiletics professor I've ever had to die a thousand deaths. ("But…she was such a *promising* student!") I mentally designated special Axe-body-spray-related punishments for every person who dared to wear cologne in my presence.

To say I was miserable was an understatement.

I don't mean to equate morning sickness with the Sufferings of the World™. On a planet wracked by famines and fires and floods, with communities upended by horrific injustices and abuses of power and illness and violence and poverty and neglect, nausea is small potatoes. It floored me, but it wasn't apocalyptic. It's not like I was dying of tuberculosis or even suffering from a chronic condition like arthritis. My discomfort wouldn't last forever—all pregnancies have a hard stop date. Still, comparing sufferings is often unhelpful, and the truth is that when you are suffering—whether it's with heartburn or divorce, terminal cancer or losing a job—comparing your pain to that of others lessens neither your pain nor theirs and generally just makes you feel lousier.

In his book *The End of Suffering*, Scott Cairns tackles this problem, framing his account of suffering first by describing the pain he felt in burying two beloved pets:

> The graves of two dogs may seem to some to be a relatively poor starting point—maybe even, to some, an insulting starting point—for this sort of inquiry. I hope not. I would never mean to equate the loss of a dog—or even the loss of two

very good dogs—with every other occasion of human suffering. Still, I would not discount how hard, how sharp, even this loss remains.[62]

If God is close to the brokenhearted, as Scripture promises, you can bet he isn't bent on deciding who is most worthy of the label before he draws near.

Perhaps most frustratingly for me as a writer, I was forced to put my experiment in spiritual disciplines on hold *again*. It wasn't a conscious choice; the words simply stopped coming. My entire life was paused. I stopped cooking and took the boys through the McDonald's drive-thru anytime Daryl was at work, breathing through my mouth until they were done with their Happy Meals. I could tell there were a couple of times that Daryl wanted to say something about the budget. He wisely kept his mouth shut. I let them mainline PBS Kids and curled into a ball at the end of the sofa, my face pressed against the window screen. Ditto on spousal silence. Church continued on as usual—one of my proudest moments was when our senior pastor told me he hadn't noticed any dip in my effectiveness at church—but when I made it home at the end of a day, I often collapsed in bed at 6 p.m. and fell asleep almost instantly. When I had the energy, I railed at God.

Couldn't you have designed a better system for bringing children into the world than this?! I asked. *What did I ever do to you?*

I agreed with Kate Bowler, who wrote of carrying her son Zach, "It was a healthy pregnancy by every standard except that I wanted to put myself in a light coma until sometime after the baby was born. *Please, anyone, surprise me with a baseball bat to the head.*"[63] To make matters worse, I often felt a great deal of self-imposed stigma that I was so utterly miserable. I shamed myself with the thought that if the baby was healthy, surely I should just be grateful—after all, I had any number of friends suffering infertility or pregnancy loss. In my exhaustion and misery I defaulted to guilt rather than self-compassion. I shamed myself for not somehow feeling happier, more grateful, more at peace with the ravages of the kind of first trimester I wouldn't wish on an enemy, much less a friend. *I shouldn't be so unhappy*, I told myself, over and over again. *This is a blessing. A gift. A…joy.*

It never seemed to occur to me that the ability to feel appreciative while leaning over a toilet bowl and saying goodbye to the little breakfast I'd been able to eat might actually be a sign of losing touch with reality rather than possessing strong Christian character. Jesus prayed, "Take this cup from me," not "Yay, Father, I'm so pumped about my impending physical suffering on the cross." Remaining upbeat in the face of such bodily misery was an unreasonable demand I would never have put on a friend in my same situation. Why *is* it that we're often our own worst critics? (And why does the voice of my inner critic sound a lot like Gordon Ramsay when someone serves him raw chicken—boisterous, male, British, and *very put out?*)

I called our birth center in desperation, where the midwives told me if I was able to keep a little food down I should be okay, and that I could try Vitamin B6 and ginger capsules and sweet orange essential oil. Sigh. They offered prescription-level big guns to quell the nausea, but neither Daryl nor I—after reading long lists of side effects and potential complications for the baby—felt peace about going that route. So much of pregnancy is enduring symptoms that would be quickly met with guns-blazing-level medications for anyone *not* serving as a transport and feeding device for a tiny human.

Migraine Headache—Not Pregnant: Here are 2,531 over-the-counter meds you can try, and if those don't work, we can put Botox needles in your brain!

Migraine Headache—Pregnant: Have you tried laying a soothing, warm washcloth on your forehead?

Severe Allergies—Not Pregnant: Here are medications, pills, nasal sprays, sinus lavages, and a billion-dollar pharmaceutical industry dedicated to making sure you stop sneezing.

Severe Allergies—Pregnant: Have you tried drinking peppermint tea? And laying a soothing, cool washcloth on your forehead?

Broken Leg—Not Pregnant: Have all the morphine you want.

Broken Leg—Pregnant: Here is some Tylenol. And also a washcloth.

To be honest, I didn't pray much. I *couldn't* pray much. I didn't write or study or read my Bible. I just existed, my body a war zone, fighting every moment to keep a little food down, to go a few hours without throwing up. Exhausted, I collapsed early every night in bed in front of streaming reality television, willing for sleep to come.

Through the fog, I began to realize on a visceral level how incredibly delicate a human person is. Something as small as a poppy-seed-sized fetus had utterly upended my life, my writing, my parenting, and my ability to be a contributing member of our household. I snapped at my kids, ignored texts from my friends, and didn't have a conversation where I was able to listen deeply and well to Daryl for months. Fast from Facebook? This little one was forcing me to fast from my *life*. And I resented it.

I preached on Sundays, sometimes leaving between the pastoral prayer and the proclamation of the Word to upturn my breakfast into the nearest bathroom receptacle, and immediately left afterward to drive home and huddle in bed, still sporting my faux pearls. Even my eyebrows got all out of control. I had nothing left to give, even to myself. It was demoralizing on a grand scale.

It was also a revelation.

Tim Keller, in *Walking with God through Pain and Suffering*, writes:

> Suffering transforms our attitudes toward ourselves. It humbles us and removes unrealistic self-regard and pride. It shows us how fragile we are.... It does not so much make us helpless and out of control as it shows us we have *always* been vulnerable and dependent on God.[64]

The reality of my suffering treated my usual disease of Can-Do-Itis and let me see myself as I really am: helpless before God. I don't know about you, but I *hate* being vulnerable, even a little. I'll go down to the honest depths with Daryl and a handful of close friends, but aside from those trusted few, I like to be the one in control: the helper, never the help-ee. The giver of grace, not the receiver of it. But in this season I had absolutely no choice. Being humbled is, well, humbling.

The close friends we'd shared our struggle with offered help with the kids and meals and errands, and we said *yes* every time. Our pride shrank until it fit in our pockets, rearing its head only once in a while to chirp, "Can't you handle this on your own?"

"Nope," we'd respond, shoving it back down.

I thought often of François Fénelon's prayer, "My God, I wish to give myself to thee. Give me the courage to do so."[65] It takes such bravery to surrender to God and others who love us, to accept a season of ineludible suffering and not fight against it, to lean into the rest that is not only offered to us but practically demanded of us when we can do absolutely no more. In these long weeks that turned into months, I could give nothing back to anyone, yet God loved me still. My boys loved me still. Daryl loved me still—and should get some sort of a medal for doing all of the cooking and cleaning and late night rock-back-to-sleep sessions and Gatorade runs ("Not *lime*, Daryl, LEMON-LIME...I'm so sorry, but you have to go back to the store.") without a single complaint for months straight. My friends reached out in compassion and kindness again and again, even though in this season they received very little from me in return. Blessed are those who leave dinner on the front steps of the barfing introvert's home, ring the bell, and drive away.

I clung to the advice Daryl gave me the week the intense nausea first began. He's seen me fight illnesses before, watched me wear myself out trying to overcome biological realities that simply don't respond to acts of the will.

"Don't fight it," he said. "Just let yourself be." I realized then that God had been working a spiritual discipline in me through this season of suffering without my knowledge or know-how. God was teaching me how to be still.

GOD OF THE HELPLESS

Stillness is hard for me. It is for many of us. To be a parent is to be in perpetual motion, caring and carrying and cleaning, changing and cajoling and cheering. To be still is to leave many important things undone, to be idle in the face of a mountain of the Necessary. I always believe that someday in the not-so-distant future I'll get better at being still, but I'd prefer it to be a choice. "God, I'll be still before you for, oh, six minutes. I give you all the time between now and when the kids wake up from their naps. I'm all yours! Do a good work in me!" Yet I *don't* do this. I refuse to choose it. But in this season, stillness was thrust upon me. Rarely is the lesson we need also the one we want.

The biblical idea of being still before God—before his will, his hand, the crucibles he uses to refine, discipline, and grow us—is a profound and age-old one. John Milton, in "On His Blindness," a poem where he wrestled with his physical limitations, writes,

> God doth not need
> Either man's work or his own gifts, who best
> Bear his mild yoke, they serve him best,
> ....
> They also serve who only stand and wait.[66]

This is radical, friends. In a consumer culture where what we do and make and create and purchase defines us, God bids us come and be.

In her beautiful book on terminal illness, Marilyn Chandler McEntyre writes, "I am gently held by the One whose light never hurts me, who knows my pain better than anyone else, and who needs no explanation."[67] God needs neither our work nor our words nor our gifts. God asks only and simply for *us*—fully given over to his loving grace. Our souls, our selves, submitted in their entirety to him. It was the evangelist Henry Varley who commented that "the world has yet to see what God will do with, and for, and through, and in, and by the man [or woman!] who is fully consecrated to Him."[68] This is one of the hidden graces of suffering: it strips us of all we are able to do until we are just ourselves, plain and unadorned, before God. Suffering disables our abilities to dress up our most base impulses—and leaves us as we are, broken people in need of a healing God.

TEMPORARY PAIN, ETERNAL GIFTS

When we shared our pregnancy news with our small group one afternoon—explaining to them why I might bolt often from the room and wouldn't be joining in for dinner—they celebrated and commiserated. And then my friend Eva said something that rang in my ears in my lowest moments of misery.

"This is temporary," she said. It is. It was. Her words might sound coldhearted, but Eva and her husband welcomed a daughter just months earlier with a serious heart defect—something they would all live with for the rest of her life. They watched her minute by minute for signs of oxygen deprivation; she'd already had one major surgery and awaited her second. It wasn't that my physical suffering paled in comparison to their knowledge that they could lose their precious baby girl at any moment (though it did, and they might), it was that their suffering was prolonged, and mine would be only a season. Even if (Lord, have mercy) my sickness continued for the entire nine months, there would be a hard stop date to it.

Temporary suffering is a unique opportunity to let God do a good work within us. The healing of a broken bone, a family stomach bug, the pain of geographical distance from someone we love…we can rail against it, or we can submit to the God who has suffered for us, continues to suffer with us, and is faithful to bring good out of the most devastating suffering of our lives. Little by little, lying in the recliner with *Master Chef* reruns, curled in bed around another glass of Gatorade, struggling mightily to remain in worship for the duration, God chipped away at my pride, my self-reliance, my lofty illusions of self-control.

In "The God We Hardly Knew," Methodist bishop William Willimon notes, "It's tough to be on the receiving end of love,

God's or anybody else's. It requires that we see our lives not as our possessions, but as gifts."[69] The unrelenting nausea brought me—quite literally—to my knees. Yet that's the posture of prayer, even when there are no words. Somehow through the haze of exhaustion and discomfort, I began to see that even my claim on my own body was misplaced. I belonged, body and soul, to God. The other thirty-four years of my life, lived almost entirely without nausea, were the greatest of gifts. The knowledge that my intense discomfort would one day soon—oh please, Lord, let it be soon!—depart was a gift as well. There was nothing for me to do but lie still, between runs to the bathroom, and let myself be loved.

So often I want to do big things for God. Grandiose things. Things that matter—as I define it. And what God desires from me—from each of us—is not more *doing*, but more obedience, even unto stillness and silence. Being on the move for God is useless if I haven't first been with God. Quaker Thomas Kelly put it this way, "Begin where you are. Obey now. Use what little obedience you are capable of, even if it be like a grain of a mustard seed....In the deeper levels of your lives where you are all alone with God the Loving Eternal One, keep up a silent prayer...'Thy will be done.'"[70]

It's one of the paradoxes of the Christian life that often what God wants from us is not for us to be on the move, doing things for him. It's for us to be with him, accepting from his hand what he has chosen for us, and allowing him to shape and form us so we will be prepared for the next action he will ask of us. It's why Jesus goes up to the mountaintop to pray—it was only in being still before his Father regularly, repeatedly, and continually that he began to be readied for his next steps.

THE GRACE OF STUMBLING BLOCKS

In college I briefly attended a Chicago megachurch. One Sunday the pastor invited people to write down prayer requests on index cards and pile them on the steps at the front of the sanctuary. After the service he asked for volunteers to stay and pray over the cards. My roommate Inga and I went to the front, gathered up a few handfuls, and prayed for each of their requests. One has stayed with me all these years.

Dear God, it said. *Please remove all the obstacles in my life so I can follow you.* Even as a nineteen-year-old it struck me as a misguided request. It is not the removing of obstacles that allows us to follow Jesus. Often the hurdles themselves are what direct us to him, press us to rely on him, and remind us of our desperate need for him. A hard lesson, but one I learned anew each morning I spent doubled over, every nap my body forced me into, and all the nights I had nothing to give Daryl but a brief hug before passing into unconsciousness.

Psalm 23 comforted me in this season, in part because, at a time when I lacked the strength of will to pick up my Bible for weeks, I knew this psalm by heart. The phrase that resounded most was from verse two: "He makes me lie down in green pastures." Thousands of words in hundreds of commentaries are devoted to the meaning of the words "green" and "pastures," but little has been written about the verb phrase "makes me." For someone on the go, rest can be elusive. Listening to God in silence and stillness and full submission feels next to impossible. But in this season? God made me lie down. Over and over again, all I had to give to him was an open hand with nothing in it at all. A clinging, grasping, begging hand. I wasn't doing anything for him. I couldn't. He had made me lie down.

And at the end of all this exhaustion and anger and lowness, as the nausea slowly lifted, I found that somehow I'd been in a green pasture all the while.

JOIN THE JOURNEY

If you aren't in a season of suffering, hooray! God isn't inviting you to join this journey today, and that's worth a prayer of thanksgiving. We work to accept suffering when it comes, but we don't ever need to seek it out.

If you are suffering, you are not alone. You are seen and loved and valued by the one who created you. Give yourself lots of kudos and all the kindness you can muster, and let God love on you. Rest in his embrace, or, if you can't bring yourself to do that (because sometimes in suffering we have many big feelings, not all of which are friendly toward God), rest on the nearest soft horizontal surface and take things one minute at a time. When you are ready—and that may be in an hour or a day or several years—invite God in anew. Being still before him is just that—being still. You don't have to do anything at all but let God love you. And when you can't do even that, God will carry you even so.

Some Scriptures that have helped me in the midst of suffering:

Psalm 23
Proverbs 3:5
Matthew 5:1–12
Romans 12:1
Revelation 21:3–6

CHAPTER 9

GETTING READY WITH GRATITUDE
Thanksgiving amid Chaos

We are people who must sing…for the sake of our very lives.
—Walter Brueggemann

Mornings are hard. They inevitably begin too early, for one thing. I'm a night owl, so anything before 9 a.m. feels cruel. Our second-born woke up at 4:45 a.m. every day for the better part of a year. *4:45 a.m.* We tried everything—later bedtimes, earlier bedtimes, two naps, one nap, brainstorming with our pediatrician. It didn't matter. Each and every morning he rattled the bars of his crib, bright-eyed and bushy-tailed at an hour when, back in my college days, I'd often just be hitting the hay. There's not enough coffee *in the world.*

Besides starting too early, mornings begin with a massive list of must-dos. There's breakfast and diapers and dressing tiny humans who would really rather not wear pants. When school's in session, there may be lunches to pack and backpacks to stuff and permission slips to sign. There are last-minute epiphanies when we remember that the library books are overdue, or we're out of toilet paper (cued by "Mommmmyyyyyy" shouted from the bathroom), or the science project is due *right now*. There are all the things we meant to do yesterday, last night, staring accusingly at us because really, who chooses *Survivor* over washing all of the dishes that have piled up? (Me. I do.)

GRATITUDE
EXPRESSING THANKS TO GOD FOR WHO HE IS
AND WHAT HE'S DONE; CONVEYING OUR LOVE
FOR HIM FOR HIS PRESENCE WITH AND
WITHIN US AND THE WORLD.

Odds are that if you're married, you live with either a Grumpy Bear or an Annoying Morning Person, and you are the opposite. For all Daryl's generally melancholy personality traits, he practically sings with joy in the morning, and I have to hold myself back from turning on the soundtrack to *Shaft*, which is absolutely the only piece of music that fits my mood before 9 a.m.

And somehow, in the swirling chaos that is morning, we adults have to figure out how to look presentable, too. Now, *presentable* can range from yesterday's hoodie to headed-to-the-boardroom-stilettos, depending on the type of work the day will involve; but no matter what, it takes work to prepare for what lies ahead.

Mornings are hard for another reason, too. No one told me that after I had a baby, I'd spend the rest of my life tucking my tummy into my pants. It's just as well. That kind of surprise is better left a surprise. Of course, there are those unicorn women who can still show up at the beach in a bikini after three sets of twins, but most of us just aren't created to carry another human inside our bellies for nine months without a single stretch mark to flag the territory. I was borderline horrified to discover that, after finally losing all the baby weight from my oldest son (which took, ahem, *years*), my tummy still looked a bit doughy and stretched out. Apparently the money I spent on prenatal belly creams and moisturizing oils would have been better spent replacing my full-length mirrors with tiny handheld ones. Have I mentioned that I sometimes struggle with body image? It isn't my greatest fight by far (see, for example, laundry), but it is something that tags along many days. I'd love to write about how I'm spiritually above that shallow nonsense, that seminary and pastoring have cured me of any focus on my outward appearance because the Lord looks at the heart and all that, but I'd just be lying to you and anyway, it's early in the morning and I'm too sleepy to be anything but brutally honest. It doesn't help that I live in southern California, home of Barbie-doll-proportioned humans, and a population that's undergone more plastic surgery (it was a deviated septum! I swear!) than what can even be remotely referred to as healthy. If comparison really is the thief of joy, my location is dangerous indeed. Yet with social media, magazines, billboards, and the like, seemingly no one on earth is immune from the pressures to look a certain way. When satellite television was first introduced to the remote Fijian island of Viti Levu in 1995, the prevalence of eating disorders more than doubled.[71] When a first-grade classmate mocked my sister's *Little Mermaid* sneakers, she never put them on again.

Beyond our bodies, women face other unique pressures to keep up with ever-shifting fashion trends. While my husband basically wears the same pair of khakis to church as when we met seventeen years ago, my pants have gone from flared to cropped to wide-leg to skinny, because that's what women's pants have done. Dragonfly jewelry was *so* ten years ago, and arrow accents are in now, but they won't be by the time this book is published. The only new addition to my husband's wardrobe in the past decade that wasn't just a replacement for a worn article of clothing was a gingham dress shirt. You guys, he's *wild*.

So between body image and fashion trends, to-do lists and lingering exhaustion, preparing for the day can feel overwhelming. Draining. Thankless. We can't retreat into stillness because there are genuinely things that must get done. If we care too much about our appearance, we may struggle with feeling silly or vapid or shallow. If we care too little, we may be offered an application for food stamps at the grocery store checkout line. (This literally happened to me my second week after moving to Orange County. Apparently wearing yoga pants on an errand only really works if they are *on trend*. Otherwise assumptions are made.)

Yet what if getting ready to face the day could be an opportunity, not for shame or hurry or frustration, but for something radically and deeply and anciently Christian? What if it was an opportunity for *gratitude*? Not a thankfulness we drum up out of thin air, by trying harder to have an "attitude of gratitude," whatever the heck that means (in general, if it fits on a bumper sticker, you can assume it's crummy theology) but one borne from giving praise to God for what he has given us—body and schedule, wardrobe and shower, kids and chaos and all.

Knowing my deep need to begin the day with a heart of thanks toward God, for this month's experiment I would practice gratitude while getting ready.

Gratitude is intimately linked to thankfulness, communicating appreciation and gratefulness for our lives. According to Adele Ahlberg Calhoun, "Delight in God and his good will is the heartbeat of thankfulness."[72]

To jog my memory—a brain function that's decidedly lower for me in the early hours—I put together a playlist of music that reminded me to be grateful. Many of the songs were explicitly Christian, but a few, like Tony Furtado's bluegrass, Tracy Chapman's rich alto, and Toto's "Africa," spoke to me of thankfulness, too. And if you can't feel at least a smattering of gratitude for the body God gave you while listening to Johnny Cash's version of "You Are My Sunshine," well, then I'll pray for you.

In the few moments in which I prepared myself for the day, I'd thank God for each step. For my body—the parts I loved and the parts I normally turned away from in the mirror. For my clothing—the new pieces and the old, those that brought me joy, and those that simply did their job in covering up all my bits. For the day ahead, whether filled or free, sunny or rainy, hot or cold. I would seek to receive what God gave as a gift, grateful to him because of who he is.

For someone who often can't form a coherent sentence until it's nearly lunchtime, this was going to be a feat of epic proportions. Or a hilarious failure. Only time would tell.

DAY 1: IN WHICH I REMEMBER BY NOON WHAT I WAS SUPPOSED TO DO

If part of practicing spiritual disciplines is failing regularly and often, then I am rocking this month's experiment already. I woke up today, dressed in a rush, and was already smearing sunblock on the kids at the park before I remembered my gratitude experiment. Clearly I'm going to need a visual aid, too.

Thankfully (ha! See what I did there?), spiritual disciplines aren't inherently *our* job. Ruth Haley Barton, in her book *Sacred Rhythms*, writes:

> The most hopeful thing any of us can say about spiritual transformation: *I cannot transform myself,* or anyone else for

that matter. What I can do is create the conditions in which spiritual transformation can take place, by developing and maintaining a rhythm of spiritual practices that keep me open and available to God.[73]

I love the idea of creating conditions. This is what we do as parents, too, isn't it? I might not read all of the top-rated books for social and mental development to my kids, but if I can create conditions in which books are readily available, reading is encouraged. And if there are fun spots to curl up with a favorite story, reading *will* happen. Barton's quote helped me shake off the guilt I'd loaded onto my shoulders this morning. Turns out grace is a lifelong lesson.

DAY 2: WE ARE OUT OF COFFEE. THE DEATH EATERS ARE COMING.

How does this happen?! We order the stuff in bulk, but somehow we're out of coffee, and even Happy Morning Husband is bumping into things in the kitchen like the Abominable Snowman in a blizzard.

Gratitude appears most easily when circumstances align. When there is enough coffee, and it is still hot. When the kids decide to play together like friends and not wild dogs. When a sunset knocks my socks off at the end of a long day. Yet, as Calhoun writes, "Thanksgiving is possible not because everything goes perfectly but because God is present."[74] This is what I'm trying to learn. Perhaps I can even find gratitude without coffee.

Perhaps. Jury's still out.

Help me to be grateful, Jesus, because right now, in this moment, I'm really, really not.

DAY 3: MATERNITY CLOTHES, COMMUNITY, AND GRACE

A couple of months ago Daryl went up to the attic to get my bin of maternity clothes. I'd saved them on a whim—we were halfway certain two kids would be our max—but now at four months pregnant, all my normal shirts had turned into crop-tops. I didn't want the upcoming Communion Sunday to turn into a Festival of Inappropriate Sharing, so it was time for the storage tub.

He carried it into our bedroom, and I popped off the lid, eager to figure out what could work for the next morning's worship service. I pulled out a pair of black dress pants, a skirt, some corduroys, jeans, shorts, more skirts, and another pair of formal pants.

"I can't believe it," I said, shaking my head. "I didn't save a single shirt." What type of dolt gives away all of their tops and none of their bottoms? She has two thumbs, and also she is me.

I put out an SOS to friends, and they came to the rescue. (Can we pause for just a moment to talk about how mom friends are the absolute best? They *get* it.) One friend who hadn't saved any maternity clothes bought me a brand new shirt at Target just to be sweet and dropped it off with a smile.

Now when I look in the mirror, I don't just see a striped top or a fuzzy sweater, I see Eva and Gail and Jessica and Carla carrying their own babies. The teal T-shirt from Annie feels like a hug every time I put it on, because it *is* one.

Thank you, Jesus, for a community of moms. For their generosity of spirit and clothing. For providing for me like you do for the lilies of the field and the birds of the air. For friends with far better taste than I have, who have not only clothed me but clothed me in items that make me feel great.

It's easy to be grateful when you have such friends.

DAY 5: BE KIND TO YOUR PASTOR

Are you a pastor? Married to a pastor? The child of a pastor? If so, you're part of a unique club: the Sunday Morning Chaos Club. Sure, getting out the door in time for church is hard with kids *period*, whether you're on a Sunday morning ministry staff or not. Everyone was up too late on Saturday or the baby didn't sleep well or you're suddenly out of oatmeal even though you could have sworn you saw plenty in the pantry yesterday. No one can ever find their shoes.

Yet for those in ministry, Sunday mornings are a time particularly prone to disaster. The preacher is all up in his or her head, parsing the finer points of Greek in the shower, trying to remember the additional worship elements—is there a baptism today, or is that next week?—doing their best to keep their nice clothes unwrinkled and free of syrup stains. But kids have these well-honed Spidey senses that immediately pick up on the lack of parental focus and turn them into tiny tornados of destruction and disagreement.

If anyone is going to get the stomach flu, it'll be in the wee hours of a Sunday morning. Repeated fire alarms, toddler nightmares, the neighbors holding a kegger? Same time. Although I lay out my clothes the night before—including accessories—on Sunday mornings, every set of earrings I own has inexplicably lost its partner. Inevitably the two-year-old, God bless him, gives me a tight hug after eating strawberry jam, smearing my last clean blazer with a sticky red trail that looks less like preserved fruit and more like something found at an LAPD crime scene. Saturday sunset to Sunday leave-for-church-time brings max chaos in the Ellis household.

I really don't mean to whine, but permit me to take things up just a notch: Daryl and I are *both* pastors. There are Sundays where—because our church holds concurrent services—we are *both* preaching. All that chaos described above? Double it. Don't get me wrong; we are blessed beyond anything reasonable to be called into such a unique and holy and rewarding vocation together. It's an absolute blast, and we wouldn't trade it for all the tea in Boston Harbor. But Sunday mornings pre-church are ca-raaaaaazy.

The congregation gathers themselves and comes to worship. We gather ourselves and our sermons and join the team that directs worship, after dropping our kids at their appropriate Sunday school stations or, occasionally, promising to lasso the moon—a.k.a., yes, you can have CHOCOLATE AND A DONUT AND A CHOCOLATE DONUT BETWEEN SERVICES—for them if they will just please sit quietly in the pew for an hour without flopping around like trout. There can be no resting crank face on the chancel, no matter how disastrously the morning may have gone. We leave behind the shaving nicks and the fights with the uncooperative hair dryer and the questions about whether one of us remembered to lock the door, unplug the iron, and turn off every light the toddler turned on (because that's his current hobby). Once we step into the worship space, it is no longer about us. There are a few hundred people ready to open the Scriptures with us, to pray and sing, each hopeful to encounter something more transcendent than their usual routine of home and work and errands and eating and bed. Easier said than done, for sure.

This particular Sunday morning went about as well as usual. Daryl was preaching today, which meant he needed enough shower time for a decent shave. (Nothing says, "Hear the Word of God" like a face covered in Band-Aids and styptic pencil...) I was still fighting severe pregnancy nausea and hence moving about as fast as a vomiting sloth. Lincoln woke up with eight million questions that need to be answered *right now. (Mommy, since*

Uncle Dave is the oldest, Uncle Dave was alone when he was born, right? But then when Daddy was born, Uncle Dave was already there, so Daddy wasn't alone, right? Mommy? And if Uncle Dave is five years older than Daddy is, how old will he be when I am six? Mommy? Mommy? Mommy?) Wilson woke up extra early after pooping through his diaper, his pajamas, and most of his bedclothes. The pancakes were burned; the coffee was cold; the kids both sported cowlicks that refused to be tamed. I couldn't find the only water cup Wilson would drink out of (the *green* one; all other colors are anathema, for a reason known only to him), and Lincoln decided to kick a soccer ball through the living room where it narrowly missed shattering a vase on the mantel. The clothes that fit me the day before didn't fit (I'm still not convinced there's only one baby in there), and I scrambled to assemble something professional-looking in forty-five seconds.

My prayers of gratitude melted into the humid morning air as we ran out the door, already cutting the time ridiculously close. As Daryl buckled the toddler in, Wilson dissolved into a puddle of tears because we locked Lambie—his rapidly graying stuffed lovie—in the house. Unlock, grab, relock. Wrong Lambie. (Yes, he has more than one. Yes, we know now that was a *terrible* idea.) Unlock, grab, relock.

I fell into the passenger's seat with a deep sigh, which was when Daryl reminded me that today was the monthly Guest Welcome Brunch between services, which means all the pastors eat and mingle in a church classroom together with newcomers and visitors. It's a phenomenal idea from our Hospitality Committee: great for outreach and connecting with guests. In this season of extreme nausea, however, it's a particularly cruel form of torture. I struggle to stomach egg casserole on a *good* day.

Thank you, Jesus. For what, I'm not sure. We are a hot mess, but I trust you're here somewhere.

I slapped on eye makeup as Daryl drove, envisioning the local paper's headline if he happened to brake suddenly, causing me to jam the mascara wand through my eyeball and into my brain.

LOCAL PASTOR GIVES HERSELF FRONTAL LOBO-TOMY. SERMONS IMPROVE.

Also, it was Mother's Day so, you know, happy that.

DAY 7: SPEEDING MY WAY TO A THANKFUL HEART

There must be a magical way to crack the code of getting kids ready and out the door by a certain time of the morning, but we haven't discovered it at our house. If you have, please write to me and, if it works, I will pay you *allthedollars*. Everyone woke up slowly today. Even Morning Guy needed a couple minutes to gather himself. There were books for the boys and coffee for Daryl (the smell of it still makes me barf, a particularly unwelcome side effect of carrying baby #3) and pancakes. The pacing felt just right, gentle and measured, but then one of us adults glanced at the clock and realized—oh my *gosh*—we had twenty-two minutes to get everything and everyone ready and out the door.

Lincoln was scheduled to be scientist-of-the-day at preschool, so being on time was paramount. In addition to his snack and backpack, there were science supplies to gather, a library book to remember, and an experiment to rehearse. Wilson slept in, which was its own dear mercy, but then he was desperate for snuggle time with Daddy while poor Daddy was trying to find a belt that matched his shoes, hopping around the bedroom with one leg in his pants.

Gratitude takes time. It takes focus. Like so many of the spiritual practices, it's hard to do on the fly. Still, I tried. *Thank you, Jesus, for these boys. All three of them, big and small. Thank you for this baby. Thank you that the pancakes are staying down. Thank you for a morning with Wilson—for his soft curls, for his wide smile. Thank you for letting me be Mom.* My shower was rushed—I had the choice of either taking a super-fast one now or a leisurely one twelve hours from now when Daryl got home from church, which was really no choice at all. I rinsed off, wondering why so much of my hair was falling out this pregnancy when I didn't lose a single strand during the last two. Might have something to do with not being able to hold down a vegetable for the past four months. Go figure.

DAY 8: TOUGH AND LASTING KINDNESS

Chuck Miller, a pastor who mentored Daryl and me years ago, was fond of saying, "God has been so kind to me." At the end of his life, his body riddled with cancer and Parkinson's, he said it just as often and meant it just as much. We thrilled on his behalf as he lit up like a Christmas tree one day in early November when, perched in front of the television, it slowly dawned on him that he was about to watch his beloved Chicago Cubs win the World Series. Simeon at the temple had nothing on elderly Cubs fans.

After Chuck's death, Daryl adopted the phrase, repeating it often to me, to the boys, to the congregation. "God has been so kind." I've begun to fold it into my mornings, praying through the ways I've noticed God's kindnesses. By naming them, I'm seeing them more often, not because life has suddenly become all rosebuds and rainbows, but because my eyes are beginning to open to the myriad ways God is working in and around me. More often than not, it brings awe. As G. K. Chesterton so eloquently put it, "Gratitude is happiness doubled by wonder."[75]

I want to learn to hold fast to God's kindness—and remember that God's kindness holds fast to me—in the good days and bad. I'm finding that God shows up just as faithfully on tougher mornings as easier ones; I only miss him because I struggle to remember to look when the day starts off difficult. Yet God's kindness runs deep. The more I tune in to hugs and breezes and oatmeal and orange juice, the miracle of being able to bear another child, the grace of pants that still fit today when every other article of clothing is in the dirty laundry bin, or even just that I made it to the sink before throwing up, the more God is glorified. He's been there all the while.

DAY 9: THE TOUGH CHOICE OF GRATITUDE

This month's spiritual practice is bringing into the light for me how very, very often I spend my morning worrying about the day ahead. Even things that don't merit real worry—run-of-the-mill meetings, well-child visits to the pediatrician, weekly grocery runs—crunch up my shoulders as I steel myself against the onslaught of the day, as if the hours themselves are after me.

Today's slate was filled with good things, yet I struggled to turn them over to God in gratitude. *Lord, help me get through that meeting. Lord, give me strength enough for the late-night young adults event. Lord, may there be nothing wrong at my pregnancy checkup.* Gratitude, it turns out, doesn't come naturally to me. I'm wired to worry. Many of us are.

As I blew my hair dry, my head bent upside down over a baby bump still small enough to bend over, I worked to turn the worries into words of thanks.

Lord, thank you for this vocation. Lord, thank you for a birth center we love and midwives we trust. Lord, I'm grateful for all the college students and young adults who are coming to tonight's event. Thank you for each one—the regulars, those who are coming home from school for the summer, the newbies, the recent graduates. Thank you for the honor of a job where I get to share your love with so many different ages. Thank you for Jordan, my co-leader, who brings the extra energy I simply don't have in this season. Thank you for Tom and Carol, who host us in their home and cook dinners for ravenous young adults. The doorknob to the bathroom rattles and wiggles, and then the door cracks open. Wilson pokes his head in, his blond hair a-frizz, his smile jolly and wide. I turn the blow dryer onto his mass of curls, and he erupts in giggles.

And thank you for this one, Lord.

DAY 10: THE DAY THAT I NEED

Back in seminary, Daryl and I interned as chaplains at a local hospital. Our little multidenominational cohort of Jews and Catholics, Episcopalians and Lutherans, Methodists and Presbyterians met together for prayer at the end of each hospital work day. We each took turns accepting night on-call shifts, so one day out of every five or so, Daryl or I would spend the night in an austere hospital apartment, waiting for the pager to ring. During the daylight hours, patients and staff called us for any number of things—to sit with a family as they heard difficult news, to pray with distraught friends in the waiting room, to read Scripture, to listen, to hold the hand of a nonresponsive patient, to keep vigil at the bedside of someone near the end of life. One doctor called me several times to visit patients who, for whatever reason, wouldn't stop crying.

"If you can't help," he said, "I'll call the psych department."

At night, however, we were only paged for one reason: death.

Serving as the night chaplain felt utterly nerve-racking, a night spent on pins and needles, professional clothing laid out next to the bed, the on-call pager set to its highest volume. Each of us interns suffered similar trepidation—we were young, inexperienced, not overly familiar with the end of life and all the raw human emotion surrounding death and dying. The hospital was eerie after hours, too: the corridors brightly lit, but the staff quiet and hushed; family members sleeping in waiting rooms; the cafeteria and gift shop and volunteer stations all darkened and closed. The more experienced chaplains—our supervisors—hid their discomfort a little better, but there were still signs. Once the on-call priest met me in the emergency department at 3 a.m. wearing two different shoes.

So as we gathered together for those holy end-of-day ceremonies in the hospital's tiny basement chapel and bowed our heads, we prayed earnestly, joined together in the solidarity of knowing what it felt like to hold on to that pager with trembling hands. Our prayers grew more personal and specific as we got to know each other, but one particular prayer began at our very first gathering and remained unchanging, night after night.

"Dear God," my supervisor Eileen prayed before Vicky—brave Vicky—took the very first on-call night shift, "please give Vicky the night that she needs." So went the prayers for each of us before we took the on-call pager. "Give Tim the night that he needs, Ramona the night that she needs, Daryl the night that he needs." On my overnight shifts I tucked this prayer into my heart, pondering it as I walked the halls, scarfed my dinner, watched *Wheel of Fortune* in the family waiting room. Could it be that amid the heart attacks and accidents and overdoses that would unfold in the hours before me, God was at work on my behalf, too? Preparing a night with not just the patients and staff, but *me*, in mind? The prayer reframed my on-call shifts from hours of dread to nights of expectation, waiting for the ways God would meet me, challenge me, and give me good work to do.

The same type of day awaits you and me today—the day that we need. Presbyterians preach about God's providence—that he holds our days, oversees our steps, weaves the threads of our moments into the tapestry of a universe far bigger and more beautiful than we can see from where we stand. As I got ready at my house on this particular morning, nearly a decade and three thousand miles removed from that internship, Eileen's prayer—one I hadn't prayed in years—came flooding back.

Thank you, Lord, for the day that I need. I haven't lived it yet, but I know you'll be with me all the while.

DAY 12: RECEIVING GRATITUDE

I was not preaching this Sunday. Neither was Daryl. Because our church holds concurrent services, unless we are away on vacation, one or both of us is *always* preaching on Sunday. Except today. A retired pastor who joined our congregation a year or so ago was bringing the word, and we got to sit together in the pews and just listen. Literally my only job was to put on a dress, bring the kids to their classes, and worship.

One of the hardest aspects of ministry for many pastors, me included, is being "on" during Sunday services. I sit up front—often on the chancel. I constantly check the order of worship to make sure I'm ready for whatever I'm about to lead—a prayer, a children's message, an announcement, a sermon. My poker face has become really, really good; I've learned not to giggle at inopportune moments, to make a mental note when something goes wrong so I can problem-solve it; to swallow any questions I have until they can be addressed later. But all of this puts a bit of a barrier between me and Jesus in Sunday worship. It's hard to pay full attention to the Holy Spirit when I have to constantly make sure my microphone is on, my skirt is covering everything it needs to cover, and I haven't misplaced the announcement flyers. This Sunday's unencumbered worship is a gift.

Practicing gratitude is slowly turning my attention to the divine more regularly. While previously I would have thought of this morning's worship in a positive light, now I see it as a direct blessing. Anne Lamott's "Thank you, thank you, thank you" prayer does wonders for the soul.[76] Even on days when I don't *feel* particularly grateful—and to be honest, I still often don't feel much of anything but grumpy in the mornings—the exercise is doing its work on my heart, drumming thanksgiving into my pulse. As Meister Eckhart noted long ago, "He knows God rightly who knows him everywhere."[77]

Thank you, Lord, for worship that happens whether I lead it or not. For Pastor Randy as he preaches. For a husband's hand to hold in the pews. For Sunday school teachers helping us train our boys in the faith. For the rare and wonderful gift this morning is.

DAY 13: RAINY DAYS AND MONDAYS

Californians are ridiculously spoiled when it comes to the weather. It's raining today, *barely* raining, just sprinkling, really, but when I popped Wilson into the stroller to run an errand, he covered his head with both hands and glared at me.

We need the rain, though, and the former Wisconsinite in me enjoys having even a little bit of weather. I love waking up to a cloudy sky. The yard shrouded in shadow gives all the greens a deeper hue, and rain brings out the smell of each thirsty flower. *Thank you, Jesus.*

DAY 14: JUST MY SIZE

Lincoln was building spaceships on the living room floor with his magnet blocks while Wilson carried big stacks of board books back and forth from the playroom, through the kitchen, and into the living room. He still barely talks, but when I came into the kitchen for a glass of water in the early hours, he looked up at me with a huge, Cheshire cat smile and said, "Hi!"

Our kids rarely wake up grumpy. Their happiness brings me happiness. It was Karl Barth who said, "Joy is the simplest form of gratitude."[78] They are grateful just to *be*. To have waffles and toy cars and blankets to snuggle with as Daryl and I start getting everything ready for the day ahead.

I tried to glom on to their joy today, but I couldn't find pants that fit when I had to be at the office in less than half an hour. Everything was either too tight or too big; for whatever reason, my maternity clothes skip right from small to large. I'm not small anymore, and I'm not large yet. The pile grew on the closet floor as I tried on pair after pair and then shed them; too big, too small, too loose, too tight. How to be grateful for this? Lying on the bed, trying to pry a pair of skinny jeans off of my pregnant calves (*why* do my legs get pregnant, too?), my eyes landed on a dress. An equal-opportunity, grow-in-girth-with-me, babydoll-style dress.

Thank you, Jesus.

DAY 17: COMPLICATED GRATITUDE

Daryl and the boys left yesterday afternoon for family camp; a long weekend up in the mountains. I'm not there; I'm at home. At my last prenatal visit, our midwife encouraged me to cut out all extraneous activities, to rest as much as possible in order to combat the unrelenting nausea. Her recommendation caused me to immediately burst into tears.

"I'm just not used to my body being so *loud*," I said. "It wasn't like this with my first two pregnancies!"

"When your body is clearly giving you such strong signals, it's important to listen," she said gently. Daryl and I went home and looked over the calendar and quickly both came to the conclusion that family camp—sleeping in a one-room cabin, walking miles a day, staying up late every night for teaching sessions—wasn't in the cards for me. So Daryl took the boys up alone. I'm hoping to drive up to spend a day with everyone later in the weekend if I'm able.

I went to bed at 7 p.m. last night and slept until 7 a.m., the peaceful, unencumbered sleep of a night alone in a usually busy house. I woke feeling better than I have in a few days: still nauseous, but almost manageably so. Then the shame started to rain down.

You're not at family camp with your family. Daryl is managing the boys all alone. The church depends on you to be there. You could have toughed it out. Why didn't you just tough it out?

As if Daryl somehow overheard the voices in my head from a hundred miles away, he texted, "Really proud of you for staying. Remember that."

Sometimes the voice of God and the voice of self-care and the voice of a kind husband are one and the same. I rolled out of bed and took a long, hot shower.

Thank you, Jesus. For Daryl. For home. For rest.

DAY 20: SOME DAYS, GRATITUDE COMES EASILY

I've found that having children leads me to awe more regularly. Sometimes it's the awe born of horror—seriously, who knew that many boogers could come out of the nose of a single toddler? More often, it's the awe that comes from the beauty and wonder of witnessing tiny people grow into bigger ones. The first time Lincoln spoke, it felt like a miracle. The first time Wilson took a step, it *was* one.

Today the not-so-small-miracle in our home is that my nausea has lifted. It's nearly all gone—there are still a few moments late at night where the idea of food turns my stomach—but for the bulk of the day, I feel okay. *Good*, even.

As Sarah Ban Breathnach wrote, "Gratitude bestows reverence, allowing us to encounter everyday epiphanies, those transcendent moments of awe that change forever how we experience life and the world."[79] After months of unrelenting queasiness, I have to believe that I will never *not* appreciate being able eat, to sleep, to cook, to come to the breakfast table with my boys. Miracles that look like a bite of scrambled eggs are no less transcendent. *Thank you, Jesus.*

DAY 22: SICK BABY, WELL BABY

Wilson woke up from his afternoon nap yesterday coughing and choking and barking like a tiny blond sea lion. In the twenty seconds or so before he could draw a ragged breath I saw the fear in his eyes; I'm sure it was mirrored in my own. Off to the children's urgent care we went. (I can count the number of times my children have gotten sick during their doctor's regular clinic hours on one finger. Praise God for a good urgent care office.) The MD on call swiftly diagnosed him with croup. Well, to be exact, it wasn't croup but "a croup-like virus," because according to the doctor, "Croup only occurs in winter."

"What's the difference between this virus and croup, then?" Daryl inquired.

"It's not winter."

"Ah."

Back at home we steamed up the bathroom and held Wilson as he worked to pull oxygen into his little lungs.

"Is he going to die?" Lincoln asked. At five years old, Lincoln is both fascinated and repelled by the idea of death.

"Don't *talk* about that," I snapped at him, laser focused on his brother.

"Oh," he said quietly. "I guess we shouldn't ever say people are going to die." Daryl, who can multitask in a crisis far better than I, moved to the sofa to gather Lincoln into his arms.

"It's okay to talk about people dying," said Daryl. "It's not bad to talk about death. But Wilson is just a little bit sick right now. He's not going to die."

This morning Daryl planned to stay home with Wilson, still too sick for the nursery at church, while Lincoln and I dressed for worship and made up over pancakes. I apologized for snapping at him the night before, but it was sitting next to him on the breakfast bench and offering extra strawberries that really won his heart back. Wilson woke late, and we all held our breath waiting for him. He coughed all night but seemed to sleep.

"Daddy?" we heard him croak out from his crib a little after seven. Daddy is his favorite right now because Mommy is getting too pregnant to toss him in the air with any regularity. We opened the door. He was standing at the rail with mussed hair and a wide grin.

There's no gratitude like the rush that comes when a sick baby—or two-year-old, but all sick kids feel like babies again to me—begins to improve.

Thank you, Jesus.

DAY 28: GRATITUDE AND GRACE

It's early June in southern California—June gloom, the locals call it. People are morose about the predictable morning cloud cover; it's often overcast until ten or eleven in the morning. Yet the clouds bring coolness, the opportunity to work in the yard without SPF 90, the chance to wear a sweatshirt. (Those of you who live in colder climes may not believe me, but I actually miss getting to wear a hoodie regularly now that I live in a desert.) I love June gloom. I wish it lasted all year. But now I'm seeing it as a unique blessing and a joy, not simply a meteorological phenomenon. God is graciously strengthening my vision for the divine. *Thank you, Jesus, for the clouds. For the cool morning. For the way the neighborhood looks different in this light, helping me to see it and my neighbors anew.*

Daryl and I do our best to give each other thirty minutes or so of uninterrupted time in the morning to go about our bathroom routines. Today as I struggled to get myself out of bed, he poked his head into the door, a grinning Wilson riding his hip.

"Take an extra fifteen minutes," he said. "I'm just getting breakfast started."

It's only Wednesday, and already we've both worked well over our part-time hours at the church. It's been a week filled to the brim with good things—initiatives and projects and meetings with leaders and shut-ins and people who need extra love and support. We've both been going to bed well past eleven, and we're tired. His gift, when viewed against the previous three days, is even bigger.

Thank you, Jesus, for a husband who sees me.

I shower, looking down at the contours of my belly, rounder every day. I can feel the baby's kicks more regularly now. The second trimester is a sweet season—I'm not too round in the middle to tie my shoes, but I'm not throwing up constantly anymore either. The walls of the shower still bear traces of the Scriptures I wrote on them months ago. *Blessed are those who hunger and thirst for righteousness, for they will be filled.*

Lord, thank you.

DAY 30: BARBARA MANATEE

Daryl says I shouldn't call myself a manatee, that this type of self-talk is "unhelpful," but I told him to try being five months pregnant at the start of a southern California summer.

"All I want to do is float in the water and eat," I said. "If that isn't manatee-esque, then I don't know what is."

We are going to the pool at the YMCA a lot these days. Lincoln is a fish, and Wilson is content to stand on the pool's stairs and pour one container of water into another for hours. Bathing suits can be a fraught article of clothing for many women, though, and I'm no exception. I remember the turning point when, at around age thirteen, swimming with my friends turned from pure frolicking to hours of holding in my stomach and trying to present my best angles. On a normal day, I'm pretty comfortable in my own skin. I can shout down the "Your Thighs Are Touching!" demons pretty well. But now I'm so very pregnant I can barely see anything below my belly button, and in the land of emaciated women in teeny tiny bikinis (can someone *please* explain to me why thong bathing suits are the new fad? I don't understand why it's suddenly considered chic to wear swim bottoms made of only as much fabric as a headband…), this is a recipe for self-hatred, not gratitude. Jesus and I need to spend a few extra minutes together before I'm ready for the pool.

Thank you for this baby girl, I say, cradling my bump. *Thank you for a body strong enough to carry this pregnancy. Thank you for this bathing suit that covers all the parts, even if I won't win any fashion awards. Thank you that there are no fashion awards at the YMCA and for helping me realize how ridiculous that even sounds. Seriously. Thank you for loving me in the midst of my insecurities. Thank you for being the God who creates life, who sustains life, who is giving me the gift of bearing another life. Thank you. Thank you.*

JOIN THE JOURNEY

When do you feel *least* grateful? For me it was early mornings, trying to get everything—and everyone—together and presentable before the day began. Maybe for you it's the end of a long work day, right before bed, or during naptime when you stew over all that is unfinished. Add in the spiritual practice of gratitude at a set time every day. Turn the negative thoughts—*I didn't, I should have, I wish I wasn't so…*—into prayers of thanksgiving. Thank God for the blessings, the hardships, the lessons, the struggles. Thank God for who he is and for who he has created you to be. Lift up the small things and the big things of your day in praise.

One final note: gratitude expands when it is shared. As often as possible, tell people about things for which you are grateful. You may find yourself surprised by the positive turns your conversations will begin to take. Thanksgiving begets thanksgiving.

Here are a few Scriptures that may help as you begin this spiritual practice:

> Psalm 105:1–2
> Psalm 136:1
> Ephesians 1:15–17
> 1 Thessalonians 5:16–18

CHAPTER 10

TRAVEL & PILGRIMAGE
Going Away and Coming Home

We are all migrants through time.
—Mohsin Hamid

I love home. Staying home, being at home, making a home. I'm a serious homebody. Perhaps my desire to be at home, to make a home, to stay at home comes from my rural Wisconsin childhood. Not only was home cozy and safe and filled with books, but there also weren't many places to *go*. In a town of 1,344 people, once school concluded for the day and hockey practice ended, my choices were limited to the forest, a friend's home, or my own. The few stores and restaurants in town closed at dusk, which fell around 4 p.m. in winter. Eagle River didn't have so much as a coffee shop until my late teens, and by then my migratory patterns were well established: school, hockey, church, home. Sometimes I'd hit up the library. Occasionally I'd get *really* wild and go hiking or cross-country skiing with friends. But mostly I stayed home.

When I began attending college in the Chicago suburbs, it surprised me that my roommates and friends wouldn't study in our dorm rooms or the library. They had this continual desire to go *out*. Out to La Spiaza, the little Italian bistro a few blocks from campus. Out to Starbucks. Out to coffee shops and libraries in downtown Chicago, each involving a Metro trip, El train ride, and long walk, often in freezing temperatures. Not to mention those who spent their summers traveling the world, participating in global missions, or studying abroad. *What,* I wondered, *was so wrong with staying home?*

Daryl experiences a bit more wanderlust than I do. He grew up in southern California, traveling across the valley for high school basketball games, taking class field trips up the coastline, and loading up the church van for missions to Tijuana. Nothing closes at 4 p.m. in Los Angeles, not even brunch places. It isn't unusual to be stuck in traffic at 3 a.m. on the 405 freeway with tens of thousands of other people, because of a good surf day or Oscar season or wildfires up in the hills. On our family Sabbath, it's Daryl who takes us out on the road. When I ask where we're headed, he smiles and nearly always says, "I'm not sure. Let's just have an adventure."

Then there are our kids, bundles of boundless energy who desire more outings than the two of us combined. Anyone who's tried to contain and entertain a child within the same four walls for more than a couple of hours knows the instant relief even a walk to a neighborhood park can bring. Travel provides a change of scenery, a breath of fresh air, a new perspective. It helps us cope with the daily grind; it readies us for what lies ahead.

Personality preferences aside, humans are created to explore, designed to adventure. It's why Magellan set sail; it's why Sir Edmund Hilary trekked up Everest. We crave new perspectives, unmet challenges, broadening horizons. Perhaps that's why when God speaks to individuals in Scripture, his first call is often for them to step out in faith, to follow a new and previously unsought path.

PILGRIMAGE
TRAVELING WITH THE AWARENESS OF THE WORK OF GOD IN THE WORLD, EMBRACING THAT THE DIFFICULTIES OF THE JOURNEY BRING UNIQUE OPPORTUNITIES TO LEARN ABOUT GOD AND OURSELVES AWAY FROM THE COMFORTS OF HOME, AND THAT ARRIVING AT OUR DESTINATION WILL PROVIDE MORE OCCASIONS FOR THE SAME.

Much of the time God doesn't even give the destination. The command is simple (and, if you're a homebody like me, perhaps a little unsettling): "Go," he says. "Go." This is God's word to Abraham, to Moses, to Elijah.[80] "Go," he says to Jonah, who runs the opposite direction and ends up smelling like sushi for a long time.[81] Simeon is "moved by the Spirit" to go to the temple, where he welcomes and blesses the infant Jesus.[82] "Get up," an angel says to Joseph in a dream, warning him to go to Egypt, fleeing from King Herod's murderous rage.[83] Yet God never asks us to do anything Jesus himself hasn't already undertaken. As Michelle Van Loon notes in *Born to Wander*, "Jesus…is calling us to un-settle and embrace a life of pilgrimage. He modeled it for us as He journeyed to the cross."[84]

So too, we parents are called to a pilgrim journey, to guide our kids as we follow God's leading, whether it's across entire oceans or just to the other side of the cul-de-sac. We are the front line of catechesis, living out the faith in the presence of our children on an hourly, daily basis. It is from us they first learn what it is to accompany our Savior on the adventures of service, study, listening, and gratitude. It is from us that they will learn if following Jesus is to be resisted and feared or embraced and celebrated.

A PILGRIM PEOPLE

While other faith traditions teach pilgrimage, Christianity has no real equivalent to this type of devoted expedition. Muslims are strongly encouraged to undertake the Hajj—a religious journey to Mecca—at least once during their lives; those who follow the Bahá'í faith are prompted to visit the Bahá'í World Centre in Haifa, Israel; Buddhists are urged to visit holy sites in Nepal or India; yet Christians tend to separate travel from spirituality. The idea of pilgrimage is not spoken about much in the church, particularly in Protestant circles. Though each year thousands of Christians travel to Israel, visiting Jesus' birthplace, the mountains where he preached, the seas where he sailed, and the hill of his crucifixion, rarely do we refer to this as a pilgrimage. Perhaps the word sounds too religious for us; maybe we think of our voyages as more educational than spiritual.

Yet Christian pilgrimage means simply to travel with our eyes open to the work of the Lord in the world around. As N. T. Wright puts it, "A pilgrim is someone who goes on a journey in the hope of encountering God, or meeting him in a new way."[85] While walking the historic roads Jesus trod during his earthly life may be a particularly stirring experience, we are also as likely to encounter Jesus in Bethlehem, Pennsylvania as in Bethlehem, Israel. It isn't that places with historic or biblical significance can't have a powerful influence on our spirits—often they can and do—it's that God is at work in and through the entire world, waiting to meet us around every corner. As our eyes begin to open to his presence, we will find him everywhere. Plus, discomfort and newness have a way of heightening our awareness, and travel brings us face-to-face with both, as when we're stripped of our comfortable routines, predictable schedules, and familiar homes, headed out on a family excursion.

IT'S A REAL TRIP

Before having kids, I had no idea the sheer amount of baggage required to take a baby any blessed place at all. Daryl and I can pack one carry-on suitcase between the two of us for a week, but now that we have kids? Forget it. A single infant needs the equivalent of a small department store just to go to Grandma's house for the afternoon. Beyond the obvious bits and pieces—diapers, wipes, bottles—there are seemingly dozens of items that aren't just nice to have along but essential for a survivable excursion. Baby has to sleep somewhere—bassinet, Pack 'n' Play, travel bed. Baby has to get from Point A to Point B, requiring a stroller, car seat, carrier, or sling. Baby has to eat—better pack the folding high chair, travel seat, clip-on booster, cup, bowl, plate, and spoon. Forget her love object of choice, and you'll wish you'd stayed home. Run out of snacks, and you'll rue the day you booked this trip. Drop the *only* pacifier on the floor during a "seatbelts please" portion of a flight, and you'll be on the receiving end of death glares from an entire plane's worth of passengers who are subjected to Baby's abject screams of displeasure.

One of my friends is fond of saying, "When you travel without kids, it's a vacation. When you travel *with* kids, it's just a trip."

Yet none of us can stay home forever—there are sights to see, places to explore, adventures to be had. Even those of us who really hate to travel—and even I, the homebodiest of homebodies, find myself desperate for a change of scenery now and then—still need to engage in it from time to time. Perhaps your extended family, like mine, is flung far and wide across the country. I'd suffer through an awful lot of car trip screaming before I'd raise my kids not knowing their grandparents and cousins. When we moved to California from the Midwest, I asked Daryl to promise that we'd travel back to my homeland annually. I wanted our boys to grow up with knowledge of the tree-laden, lake-studded landscape that shaped me; with memories of their grandparents and great-grandparents; with an understanding of the reality that most of America is not twenty minutes from an ocean. I needed for them to touch the snow.

Plus, travel rejuvenates. Even on our shoestring budget, Daryl and I found that just a couple nights at a campsite can reinvigorate our parenting and our marriage and our souls, simply because we've been able to look at our lives from a new perspective for a while. (And also more fully appreciate the miracle that is indoor plumbing.)

Whether we fly across the country or simply drive an hour to visit a friend, travel provides us with a unique opportunity to experience God anew by approaching our journey not just as travelers but pilgrims—people on the lookout for God at work and opportunities to join him. Jesus was the ultimate pilgrim, after all—leaving his heavenly climes to not only visit with, but to live among, humanity. He faced all the usual obstacles to comfort that plague us when we travel—difficulties in finding food and shelter, misreading the vibe of a particular place, having to rely on the hospitality and grace of strangers and family and friends. "Foxes have dens," Jesus said, "and birds have nests, but the Son of Man has no place to lay his head."[86] Jesus leans into this discomfort, the necessity to rely upon the kindness of those we meet along the road, telling his disciples to "take nothing for the journey."[87] He invites us to do likewise. (Though, to be fair, none of the disciples was toting a two-year-old. Surely then even Jesus would have advised bringing an extra snack or two.)

Away from our usual environment, at the mercy of the road or the airlines or the weather or the host home, we are given the opportunity to see the world with new eyes: to receive welcome, to develop compassion, to grow in faith and trust that God will care for us throughout the journey and see us safely home at its end. For a Christian, travel is not simply getting from Point A to Point B; it is an occasion for pilgrimage.

THE JOURNEY BEGINS

In our upcoming summer travels, I will seek to practice pilgrimage, watching for God as our family journeys, looking for opportunities to love those in my path with the love of Christ, and doing my best to accept discomfort and even disaster as means of discipleship and grace. To mark the time, we will begin our travels with a family prayer, inviting each member to ask God for their desires for the day. When we arrive, we will thank God together as a reminder of his presence with us along the way.

This month's practice is well-timed: our little family heads toward some pretty big travels over the next four weeks. The first excursion is just a day's jaunt up to Los Angeles to visit Daryl's side of the family: brunch and then a retirement party. It's a warm-up trip to help us prepare for the real marathon: flying back to the Midwest for our annual tour of family, an excursion which involves waking the kids at 4:30 a.m., utilizing a ride-share service, getting on and off two different airplanes with approximately sixty-eight pounds of gear and car seats and strollers and enough snacks to make it up and down Annapurna, and then enjoying a week in the northern woods of Wisconsin before buckling up for an over eleven-hour drive to Michigan, where we'll hang out for another week with more than forty extended family members before taking a connecting flight home at an ungodly hour of the morning, landing only a few hours before I preach on Sunday. We look forward to our midwestern pilgrimage all year long, and also, it is definitely a trip.

Pray for us.

DAY 1: FIRST, A SHORT TREK

We drove the sixty-five miles up to Los Angeles and then back again today. Daryl's family is spread across the San Fernando Valley, and we try to see them when our free Saturdays coincide. As a person raised in rural America, it always baffles me that a simple sixty-five-mile drive can take anywhere from an hour to four hours or more depending on traffic. Locals here talk about highway congestion like Wisconsinites and Michiganders and Minnesotans talk about the weather: with passionate frustration and unsolicited advice.

"Oh, you took the *405*? Well, there's your problem. It always backs up around Inglewood. What you *should* do is get off at the 5 and take that to the 101 and avoid Santa Monica entirely. If it backs up in Sherman Oaks you can take Ventura Boulevard. Plus, there's an In-N-Out Burger just after Oakdale, so, you know, it's like totally worth it." My first years in California I'd just nod and smile as this barrage of information came at me, making about as much sense as high school physics to an English literature aficionado. California traffic patterns are not my first language.

Today's trek took only an hour and fifteen minutes. Making it in such a short time felt akin to dividing the Red Sea (of traffic), a borderline miracle in the land of bumper-to-bumper-doesn't-begin-to-describe-it. The kids were troupers, both browsing through books in the backseat—Lincoln reading and Wilson pretending to read because his heart's desire is to do absolutely everything his brother does. I planned to work on a writing project as Daryl drove, but the combination of a late night, a coughing kid in need of soothing (it was my idea to use local honey as a natural, low-grade expectorant, and now whenever he has the sniffles Linc basically turns into Winnie the Pooh), and an early morning had me passed out in the passenger's seat before we even pulled onto the freeway. No one ever told me to marry the guy who likes to do almost all the driving, but *man*, it's quite a perk.

Blessing though it was, our quick drive time meant no one was ready to meet us when we arrived, because they assumed we'd be late. LA traffic trains people to add thirty minutes to every projected arrival time, and give grace periods of up to ninety. My punctual German ancestors wouldn't handle it well. We pulled in to meet Daryl's mom for brunch at a popular spot in Burbank only to find a line snaking around the outside of the restaurant all the way to the street. Luckily Grandma Sylvia is a public librarian who always comes prepared. Three Berenstain Bears books and an Amelia Bedelia later, we were seated.

"Who wants whipped cream on their waffle?" asked Daryl, and the table erupted in a chorus of cheers.

"Me!" yelled our two-year-old, flashing a giant grin about both the whipped cream and his fledgling vocabulary, thumping his little chest with a finger. "Me! Mine! No, me!"

As the kids polished off their breakfast, along with numerous jam packets because, in kid logic, anything placed on the table by the restaurant is fair game (not a totally crazy thought, I suppose), I leaned back in my chair, sipped my orange juice, and enjoyed

184 ALMOST HOLY MAMA

the blessing of not being the only adult in charge. Burbank is central to "the industry" in Los Angeles—local parlance for the television and movie business—and the diner was packed with a mixture of young families like ours, parents and grandparents just grateful for someone else to provide coffee and clean up breakfast, and Hollywood professionals eating egg-white omelets, wearing dark sunglasses and jeans that cost more than our car. California is a study in fascinating contrasts.

It's taken us years to work out, but after eleven-plus years of marriage, Daryl and I now know it's wisest to let him handle the logistics when we travel to visit his family; likewise, I handle the schedule and planning when we head back to the Midwest. These trips bring out the differences in our methods (I plan ahead, while Daryl enjoys serendipity; I prepare for every eventuality, while he prefers to throw a few diapers and a bag of tortilla chips in the car and hope for the best), but since the Ellis side of the family lives in a thriving metropolis close to all manner of convenience stores and restaurants, I'm learning to hang loose on these local treks. How very Californian of me! As these drives to Los Angeles become more common, God is faithfully teaching me that my rigid, planned-up-to-the-minute travel method isn't always the best one. In fact, the biblical model for following Jesus is much more Spirit-led than plotted in advance.

It isn't that preparation isn't necessary or helpful—one time we visited our Wisconsin pediatrician without a change of clothes for infant Lincoln, and of course he pooped up his back and had to ride home wearing only a diaper and a snowsuit—it's that openness to the Spirit of God is more important still. "The wind blows where it wills," Jesus tells Nicodemus in John's gospel.[88] Paul's journeys were continually interrupted by storms, bandits, imprisonments, and mobs; and once, when he made it all the way to the outskirts of the province of Asia, the Spirit of God turned him away at the last minute.[89] God invites us to plan and prepare—kids need supplies, everyone needs snacks—and then to step into the footprints of a pilgrim, eyes opened for whatever he might have in store.

God is much more interested in growing our trust in his provision than in abiding by the precision of our spreadsheets. I'll admit that I would not have handled God's stern prohibition against saving manna in the desert very well (I need to PLAN!), and perhaps God is using Daryl's variant personality type—which differs vastly from my own—to teach me this, too, as we practice pilgrimage together as a family. He's got a great handle on hanging loose and trusting God with the day ahead, and I have much to learn from his willingness to go with the flow, eyes opened to opportunities, detours, and moments of grace.

DAY 5: VACATION BIBLE SCHOOL, AND OTHER THINGS WE BARELY SURVIVE

It's VBS week at our church. This means hundreds of kids will play games, make crafts, meet new friends, and learn Bible stories. Some will hear the gospel for the very first time. It also means that anyone volunteering for VBS—including my husband and me—will be absolutely ready to sleep for a month by the week's end. Even our usually unbelievably energetic twenty-three-year-old associate youth director is dragging a bit. She texted me yesterday: *I took three naps.*

We may only be traveling the five miles to church and back home each day, but everything that happens between dropping the boys with their teachers and picking them up three and a half hours later is a pilgrimage indeed. Enthusiasm, cheer, problem-solving, question-answering, skit-performing, volunteer-encouraging. Daryl's leading a crew of four-year-olds; I'm writing and performing in the skits and stepping into whatever other gaps present themselves, which, with a volunteer program this size, are *numerous*.

By Thursday we're all creaking and groaning like ninety-year-olds when we try to get out of bed to start another day.

"I'm sick," Lincoln told me, hanging his head low and dragging his feet.

"Which part of you doesn't feel good?" I asked. He sighed and gestured broadly from his head to his toes.

"Alllll of this," he said.

"I think you have a case of VBS-itis," I said. "But don't worry. Daddy and I have it, too. The only way to cure it is to sleep in on Saturday and eat donuts and watch the World Cup."

I'm amazed at my own capacity to drag my feet this week. When exhaustion hits, my compassionate side—the one that notices Daryl's fatigue, that takes an extra moment of tenderness to snuggle the tired boys and find the "right" Lightning McQueen Band-Aid for an invisible owie ("No, not that one, Mommy, the *other* one with Lightning on it"), that remembers to clear a path in the toy detritus between the living room and the bedrooms so no one steps on a Lego while trying to refill a water cup in the wee hours—is nowhere to be found. This isn't sin. We aren't robots, after all. There's no magic button we can push when our tank *and* our reserves are on empty, no special super-secret level of functioning we can access to become superhuman, overriding our own creatureliness. Practicing pilgrimage doesn't mean ignoring our own needs, the ache of our souls, the weariness in our bones. Part of being set in a family is learning to lean on one another—

and together on God—in strenuous or stressful times, and to give each other buckets of grace when the whole household is at its end. Character is forged in the fire as exhaustion brings us to our knees, to our beds, to our couches and our floors, learning to love each other and ourselves as best we can with the little we have as we wait to be filled back up by sleep and nourishment and the untiring, unending love of Jesus.

Michelle Van Loon notes that this realization is an integral part of pilgrimage. "We may have responded to the call to follow Jesus and start walking. But the deserts in our lives are where we begin to discover how to follow God even when—especially when—our circumstances don't make sense."[90] One of the most insidious temptations of ministry is to give it our all while reserving nothing for our families. Countless pastors have fallen from grace after leading thriving congregations but neglecting their marriages, their children, and even their own souls. The call of God to serve a congregation or a parish, a denomination or a nonprofit ministry, is never the call to attend to a worshiping body at the expense of our families. And the call to serve our families is never a call to work for them at the cost of our bodily or emotional or mental health.

Even the intensity of Vacation Bible School is no excuse for me to shove my kids or my soul aside because "ministry," but it *is* an opportunity to drink from the unending well of living water that goes infinitely deeper than my own little sippy cup of mothering endurance. So today I begged God for an extra measure of grace and energy and patience, because I'm out of each of them, and he met me in that low place with not only each of these but early bedtimes for all, too.

All the praise hands.

DAY 8: NOW WE PACK

People tend to fall into one of two categories when it comes to preparing for a trip. Type A are those who make checklists and begin planning days ahead of time so they can make umpteen runs to Target and the grocery store and the pharmacy, making sure they have every little thing they could possibly need, and it's all properly organized. This is me. I'm a disorganized disaster in my normal life, but when there is a trip on the horizon, I turn into a human spreadsheet. Perhaps it's that I've taken so many trips with small children. Maybe it's because I have eating restrictions and need to bring my own food everywhere, which takes foresight. It's definitely not that I have control issues because I DON'T HAVE CONTROL ISSUES, YOU HAVE CONTROL ISSUES.

Type B is comprised of those who take a laissez-faire approach to the whole thing. They throw some stuff in a bag on their way out the door and figure that since they aren't blasting off into outer space, they will eventually stumble upon a Walmart to pick up whatever they forgot. Odds are, if you are a Type B, your spouse is solidly in the Type A camp. God does this to us to make us holy. Or else insane.

Now, to be clear, Daryl works harder than anyone I've ever met. He's our resident kitchen cleaner; he offers to change every diaper that gets soiled while he's within shouting distance. Not to mention that he does the laundry and most of the driving, too. He finished a dissertation while working as a pastor and still read the boys bedtime stories almost every single night. He's building a shade structure for our backyard from scratch— including pouring concrete and welding steel—with help from a church friend.

But when it comes to packing, I feel the urgency days in advance, and he simply doesn't. While I run around making lists and pulling backpacks from closets and making sure we have exactly the right combination of books and action figures and travel games for the kids so they don't get so stir-crazy they start gnawing through their armrests, Daryl sends emails. While I fold laundry and search for missing shoes and measure all of our liquids and gels to make sure they are the proper size, stuffing gluten-free granola bars into every suitcase nook and cranny, doing advanced calculus to determine how many diapers we will need, and stockpiling Children's Tylenol because the one time we forgot it Lincoln spiked a fever in an airplane over Omaha and it was *the worst*, Daryl checks ESPN.com again because maybe some big sporting thing happened in the eight minutes since he checked it last. There have literally been days when we need to leave the house to catch a plane by 5 a.m., and while I'm in the shower at 4 a.m. I suddenly hear the washing machine start up, because *in his mind an hour is the perfect amount of time to clean that shirt he wore yesterday and wants to take on the trip.*

I love Daryl with the fire of a thousand suns, but when I hear that sound—*whoosh, whoosh, spinnnnn*—in my groggy it's-still-dark-out-and-we-have-a-twenty-hour-day-ahead-of-us state, I contemplate all the ways I could kill him without leaving behind any evidence. He is basically perfect and I totally adore him, but if we traveled more often, you might very well see me on *60 Minutes*.

You may imagine that nearly all of our family vacations are preceded by marital fights. Aaaaand you'd be correct.

Perhaps the best spiritual lesson pilgrimage offers is the lesson of silence, of being quiet when we want to be right, and instead letting small annoyances or injustices slip from our minds while we allow the day to continue to unfold. As Paul writes so beautifully, "Love suffers long."[91] Daryl and I used to burn all of our energy for the travel ahead hashing out why each other's bizarre packing habits filled us with rage, why we were right and the other was so very, very wrong, but over the years God has begun to graciously help us hold our tongues more and more; to wait for the initial ire to fizzle; to say *thank you* for the little things we both do that warrant gratitude; and to start the day on a kinder and softer note.

James puts it this way: "Everyone should be quick to listen, slow to speak and slow to become angry."[92] We work hard for this. Little by little we are growing in it. Sometimes, of course, we fail. We snap, we grumble, we start the day with fire instead of grace. But the good news of travel is that the days are long, and we will have time to apologize and start anew, not to mention many more opportunities to learn these particular lessons of patience and silence, if we're willing to learn them.

DAY 9: WE WILL GET THERE OR DIE TRYING

It was 5:22 a.m., and we were off to the airport. Daryl performed the last of his eighteen double checks. (Is the water off? Are all the doors locked? Do we want the outside light on? Did we remember to take the goldfish to the neighbors' house?) I made sure all the kid snacks and distractions were at my fingertips in my carry-on. We loaded up just twenty-two minutes past when we intended to leave. That might be a record. In a good way.

With the kids strapped into their car seats in the back of a Lyft—by some miracle we got the four of us, two car seats, three suitcases, a stroller, and two backpacks into a Toyota Prius— Lincoln chattered away at Bill, our driver, while Wilson half-dozed with a residually sleepy grin. Daryl was sweating like he just completed an Olympic triathlon; my hair was still wet from the shower; Lincoln's socks didn't match; but we'd *made* it. We were buckled in, and all systems were go.

The sky began to brighten as we drove. Our driver turned the air conditioning on full blast in the humid California morning. Daryl checked and double-checked our flight time, his phone, his wallet. He asked me, for the second time, if I had my driver's license. Things were, for the moment, going okay. I savored it. Thank you, Jesus.

There was no way this would last.

DAY 9 (CONTINUED): AT THE AIRPORT

I tried not to stare at the massive clock hanging just over our heads as the security line shuffled forward at a snail's pace. I thought we'd left the house with time to spare, but I was sadly mistaken. My heart began to pound; with each moment that ticked away, the chance we wouldn't make our plane increased.

The TSA lady at the airport watched Daryl and me juggle two kids and their myriad accoutrements at 6:03 a.m., and noticed Wilson burst into tears when Lambie left his arms to travel through the scanner.

"Do you like stickers?" she asked him. He paused his wail to study her. She just took his love object away to put it on a conveyor belt, so clearly she couldn't be trusted, but people in uniform are usually too busy to talk to a two-year-old, so he was intrigued. "Watch for your lamb," she said, leaning over the belt to look Wilson in the eye. "He's coming right back, and when he makes it through the scanner, he will have a surprise for you." Wilson sniffled and clung to my shoulder with both pudgy hands. Sure enough, when Lambie made it through, he was wearing a

TSA junior agent sticker, with another in his paws for Wilson. Just as Lincoln piped up in protest—he may feel too old for stickers, but he's certainly not too old to feel left out—the agent leaned across the line and handed him one of his own.

"Safe travels," she said with a smile.

We scrambled back into our shoes and backpacks, plunked Wilson into the stroller, and sprinted to our gate. There was no one there but a single attendant.

"They've already boarded," she said. "You're just in time. Go right on."

Settling into our seats, I was bowled over by the unexpected kindnesses of the morning. We travel often enough that I've learned to anticipate business-as-usual at the airport at best, and nonsensical crankitude at worst. On our last flight with Wilson, an irate, impeccably dressed businesswoman in the row behind me yelled at us to "just swaddle him already." The airline had changed our flight at the last minute to take off an hour *after* his bedtime, leaving us with nothing to do but try our best to endure the exhausted-toddler chaos. Musician Nicole Nordeman wrote on Twitter about how her kids are grown now, but every time she flies she feels deep compassion for those traveling with littles. I shared my story, and she responded, "Swaddle a 2-year-old. No problem. Pardon me, ma'am, could you hold my drunk German Shepherd? A lullaby, perhaps?"[93]

Last night at college group, a guy in my prayer circle asked God to surround my family with kind people on our upcoming travels. I realized then—and it hit me again as I boarded our plane this morning—that this is the key to a smooth journey. Not that the road would be easy; not that the airport would be free from hassles; not that we would face no inconvenience or frustration or trouble; but that in the midst of all these things, there would be kindness. It's only 6:47 a.m., and already God's kindness has surprised us by showing up in spades.

Perhaps the most beautiful quality of mercy—from God or others—is that it shows up where we don't expect to find it, making a home for us where we thought we'd be strangers. As Anne Lamott writes in *Hallelujah Anyway*, "Just to hear the words 'mercy' or 'merciful' can transform the whole day....We know mercy is always our salvation."[94] The strange ability of a simple smile or a sticker, a Lyft driver skilled at suitcase Tetris, a hand waving you onto a plane you thought you'd missed, or a path slightly smoother than you had feared it'd be to bring you face-to-face with God, is nothing short of miraculous.

In case you were wondering, Jesus is still Lord at the Santa Ana airport.

DAY 9 (CONTINUED): THE SECOND FLIGHT

For all the kvetching people do about how screens are ruining the brains of an entire generation, when I am on an airplane with my children, I'm so grateful for digital distractions I could kiss Steve Jobs right on the mouth. (Back when he was alive, of course.) I've lost count of how many episodes of *Veggie Tales* and *Octonauts* Lincoln watched today, and frankly I do not even remotely care. As long as his headphones were working, he was so quiet and still I almost forgot he was there.

Wilson, on the other hand, could care less about screens. We got him to watch *Cars* for approximately fifty-eight seconds, but after that he shoved my phone away and began looking for a new diversion. Daryl and I juggled him between us—now that Wilson is two years old, he requires his own plane seat, but it's easier to hold and snuggle him after the seatbelt sign goes off than to listen to him wail. While Daryl held him, I dozed for a few moments; then it was my turn. You never realize how big your kid is until you try to hold him on your very pregnant lap in a tiny economy seat.

A drunk German shepherd indeed.

DAY 9 (CONTINUED): ARRIVAL

As our plane descended over the green forests and blue-black lakes of northern Wisconsin, I pointed out the topography to Wilson. He slammed his window shade shut and cackled. *This* game was more fun than staring at trees. My soul exhaled with the realization that we were nearly there. Grandparent reinforcements were close at hand.

As soon as we disembarked, the kids ran across the tarmac, to the terminal, and into my dad's arms.

"Pa!" Lincoln exclaimed.

"Pa!" Wilson echoed, not to be left out. We hugged and grabbed suitcases and headed out in a light drizzle to the car. When it was time to replace my parents' main vehicle a couple years ago, they passed right by the sedans to purchase a minivan so they could help haul the grandkids.

"Are you guys thirsty?" My mom passed back a bottle of water for each of us as I melted into the backseat. We'd made it. Praise the Lord and *pass the naps*.

DAY 10: WHAT A TRAVEL HANGOVER TAUGHT ME ABOUT GRACE

As one who is more bear-straight-from-hibernation than actual human before 9 a.m., I'm embarrassed to admit that it's mostly guilt that gets me out of bed in the morning. Guilt that

Daryl is managing two kids and breakfast on his own. Guilt that I'm cozy in bed when the day is starting. Guilt that even though he's Morning Guy, he still needs a bathroom break and a shower, both of which are far easier with a second parent who's vertical.

But the late morning after our arrival I was still in bed, wrapped in a cocoon of down comforter and oversized pillows. I had no earthly idea what time it was, and I didn't care. My parents had been dying to spend time with their grandkids for months, and though I could tell by the angle of the sunlight sneaking through the shades that I'd slept until nearly the afternoon, the house beneath me sounded empty. I rose slowly, the aches of a third trimester and a long day of flying gripping my back, my belly, my legs. In the bathroom I met Daryl brushing his teeth, two days' worth of stubble helping him look more like a Wisconsin local and less like a guy from Los Angeles.

"I'm just going to take a quick shower," I began, ready to launch into my usual morning spiel, the one about how I need just a couple more minutes before I'm ready to face the day. He stopped me with a hand on each shoulder.

"We're on vacation," he said. "Your parents have the kids. No hurry *at all.*"

What is it not to hurry? Our life is so scheduled, so fine-tuned to keep the church on track, to make it to appointments, to get Lincoln to his swim lessons and the kids to Sunday school and all four of us and the house presentable before our next event. We've done a lot of work in the past couple of years to avoid overscheduling, to leave room for breathing and downtime and play, but even those chunks are religiously planned, because without foresight, all the hours fill.

One of the lessons God offers to us in travel is to find peace amid the storm—the chaos and scramble of getting from Point A to Point B with kids in tow. But another lesson is to embrace stillness and slowness when it comes, to not drag the intensity of our work lives and activity schedules and kid pandemonium into the quieter days of travel. Often it is in a new setting, far from the everyday stressors and pressures of home, that we begin to see God anew as we welcome the slower hours and days God offers to us. As Carlo Carretto puts it, "That is the truth we must learn through faith: to wait on God. And this attitude of mind is not easy. This 'waiting,' this 'not making plans,' this 'searching the heavens,' this 'being silent' is one of the most important things we have to learn."[95]

I relish these times in the Northwoods, not solely for the time spent with family, but also because they force me to slow down. Not just by sleeping in—though I couldn't possibly be more grateful for these extra hours of recovery—but by a whole host of delightful inconveniences that feel engineered to help me unplug. My parents' internet is spotty; my cell phone works only intermittently; the last time I heard a siren of any kind was at the town Fourth of July parade half a decade ago. Back home, Daryl and I often fall asleep watching *The West Wing* or *The Office* in an effort to still our ping-ponging thoughts. Here, any digital streaming takes literal hours to download, so we simply don't. At night we open the windows to hear the oak and maple leaves blow in the wind, falling asleep with books on our chests.

When we spend these days in the quiet of the northern forests, it's as if Jesus stands at the helm of our proverbial boats during the storm of the usual daily grind—ministry, school, appointments, errands, household chores—and says, "Peace. Be still." "Sweet Jesus," poet Mary Oliver calls him. "Talking his melancholy madness."[96]

In these pilgrimage moments, I'm ever so slowly learning to listen.

DAY 15: THE LONG, LONG DRIVE

I never realize how easy my day-to-day life is until I'm in transit. Of course, my daily existence isn't all bonbons and pedicures (in fact, it's exactly *zero* bonbons, and I literally get one pedicure a year and it's *for my birthday*). Yet in an average day, I am able to eat when and what I'd like, sit somewhere comfortable, and enjoy long stretches of time where I control everything from the lighting to the music to the temperature. But, parents? Plunk yourself down in any road trip vehicle, and suddenly it's not all about *you* anymore. There are other people—spouse, kids, maybe relatives or friends, too—who have needs. They prefer the temperature to be six degrees hotter than the Kalahari Desert; they need stretch breaks *way* too often; they monopolize the sound system with *Veggie Tales* or Van Halen. Travel forces us immediately into our new role as Team Player™ when we are normally used to calling the shots.

For our annual drive from my parents' home in Wisconsin to our family reunion in Michigan, six of us—seven, if you count the baby girl who's recently turned head-down in utero and keeps a sharp heel jammed into my rib cage to remind me—piled into a minivan pulling a U-Haul trailer filled with beach gear and suitcases. Tonight we'll be met in Chicago by three other adults and three more kids before meeting up in Michigan with the rest of the family. The four of us adults are trying to get along when the morning has already been a jumble of differing opinions and competing needs. I've situated my pregnant self in the very back row of minivan seats. This was a bad decision; I already have to pee.

I wonder whether our obsession with making everything more convenient, faster and slimmer and more prepackaged, actually grows from our resistance to accommodating one another and the growth it offers to us. *Faster, higher, stronger* isn't a slogan that shows up anywhere in Scripture. Instead Jesus talks of the faithful planting of seeds, the slow growth of crops, the patient and predictable turning of the seasons. Slow and steady and inconvenient and good. As William Willimon notes, "This is often the way God loves us: with gifts we thought we didn't need, which transform us into people we don't necessarily want to be."[97]

Speaking of inconvenient, one of the difficulties of traveling with kids is they are immobilized much of the time, and immobilized little ones get bored *fast*. Bored kids need diversions, else the vehicle quickly fills with the dull roar of frustrated toddler and equally frustrated mom. As the parent who usually copilots the car, the distractions most often fall to me. Our toddler isn't very interested in the magical world of Netflix yet (a fact we are usually quite smugly proud of, but on trips I'd really like him to be a bit more engaged with *Daniel Tiger* so Mommy could do a crossword puzzle and take a nap). Since digital distractions are no distraction to Wilson, he still needs constant attention—a book, a puzzle, a new song on the radio, a snack, a snack, a snack. At home he'll pull out his magnetic blocks and entertain himself for a half hour at a time. While traveling, we often get on a five-minute loop where he looks at a picture book and then chucks it to the floor. Plays with some action figures, then chucks them to the floor. Eats half an applesauce pouch and then—well, you guessed it.

If patience is learned in small, repeated increments, then this drive is shaping up to lead me to sainthood.

DAY 16: I'M NOT STEERING THIS CAR

My dad is a good and steady driver who hauled our entire family across the country a dozen times when I was a kid, handling blinding hailstorms and pouring rain and extreme blizzard conditions, managing mountain switchbacks and mesmerizingly boring desert flats, and swerving around half-a-dozen-car pileups without breaking a sweat. Yet anytime I'm a passenger in my dad's car, I feel a rising tide of panic.

It started when I was a kid. My sisters would sleep or read or play travel games, and I'd stare numbly out the window, watching the road, because if I didn't, we might have an accident. I don't know where the thought came from, but somehow I felt responsible for the whole car. Arriving at our destination, my sisters would have boundless energy and I'd be utterly drained, my body aching from hours of tensed muscles from my backseat vigil.

Early on in our marriage, Daryl noticed I carried this bizarre self-determined car trip responsibility.

"You can nap, you know," he said once, raising an eyebrow at my ready-to-spring position in the passenger's seat. "Or at least lean back in the seat a little bit."

As a passenger, I control nothing about the car's speed or trajectory, yet I feel all the responsibility in the world, like it's my job to will the car to stay in its lane, avoid accidents, and keep to the speed limit. I don't say anything—verbal backseat driving isn't my style—but I'm on high alert just the same. This bizarre, self-imposed lookout signals a lack of trust in the driver, which would be one thing if that driver was a bad one, but I generally ride with people who have proven nothing but capable. This lack of trust, desire for control, and belief that if I just concentrate fiercely enough I can steer things any direction I want them to go is an apt metaphor for my spiritual life as well.

Anne Lamott has this great passage in *Operating Instructions* where she writes of a prominent doctor she heard speak:

> He said that when he sees little kids…in those car seats that have steering wheels, with grim expressions of concentration on their faces…he thinks of himself and his relationship with God: God who drives along silently, gently amused, in the real driver's seat.[98]

Maybe you struggle with this same unhealthy desire for control. Or worse yet, perhaps like me you struggle with the misguided belief that you *are* in control, that if you simply concentrate hard enough or plan far out enough or anticipate every eventuality, you will never again face an accident or an obstacle or even a serious inconvenience. It's a rough way to live, friends, and not the path of faith and trust in the one who guides and guards our steps.

Pilgrimage brings this lack of faith to the surface for me in a way that stings a bit; truth often does. Sometimes the correction of God burns like iodine in a scrape as it brings our attention to an area of pride, of sin, of selfishness, of distrust. According to Proverbs, "the Lord disciplines those he loves."[99] God seeks to peel our fingers off our metaphorical steering wheels, not in cruelty, but in order to free our hands to receive his peace, to learn to hold on to his strong hand with trust, to be freed to reach out to others, and to undertake the pilgrimage he sets before us with joy.

This trip, that looks like a lot of deep breathing in the backseat, and a lot of prayer. After three decades of believing I need to steer the car, this one's going to take some time to unlearn. *Help me, Jesus.*

DAY 20: CREATURES OF HABIT

It's our fourth day at our family reunion at a conference center on the shores of Lake Michigan: all forty-some of us, from the newest (three months old) to the oldest (my grandparents, now in their mideighties). When I tell friends we have a weeklong family reunion, many of them respond with sympathy; but really, we look forward to this week all year. It's a combination of catching up with far-flung relatives (at last count, we were spread over ten states from the East Coast to the West), returning to childhood (it doesn't matter that we're sleep-deprived parents, we *will* stay up way too late playing Mafia), and reconnecting with our own nuclear families far away from work responsibilities. The conference center also has *killer* children's programming, which never hurts.

Lincoln and Wilson are over-the-moon enraptured by our environs, loving the occasionally rainy Midwest, the cooler temperatures, the crazy-big spiders that line the patio every morning, the wild Lake Michigan waves. Lincoln braved the zip line this year, and Wilson is learning to climb the pool ladder to jump into the arms of a waiting grandpa or aunt. We're surrounded by cousins galore, and after meals the kids play Wiffle ball and soccer in the field out back, tumbling around on the grass, getting delightfully summer-dirty.

The change in routine is both a joy and a strain. Three time zones out of our normal rhythms and at the mercy of the conference center's schedule means that naps are earlier and bedtime is far later. Yesterday afternoon Lincoln came into the room, laid his face on our bed, and proclaimed, for the first time in his entire five and three-quarters years of life, "Mommy, I am *really* tired." Today I had to pry him out of his bed for breakfast like a surly teenager. I fluctuate between being amazed by the kids' flexibility—the pool closed for a filter change yesterday, and after a moment of pouty-lip, Wilson rallied admirably—and exhausted by their constant negotiations. Freed from the structure of the daily grind—library on Monday, laundry on Wednesday, groceries on Friday—we have critical distance to see what was working and what needs more thought. But it's also those same, regular routines of home that free us from the exhaustion of having to debate each of the day's activities.

Still, the thousands of decisions we face in travel are unique opportunities to meet with God, to be flexible, to let others lead. I'm learning to let little things go, if only because there are so many little things in this week that I can't possibly keep them all in hand. The ups and downs of a week overflowing with extended family—each person with a unique personality, particular needs, a story to share—are helping me take each moment as it comes …which is, in a way, the lesson of relying on God I need most. To welcome conversations and solitude, laughter and tears, later bedtimes and earlier naps as I can—and when I can't, to ask God for daily bread.

DAY 21: UNPLUGGING IS HARD—AND WORTH IT

Daryl and I worked relentlessly before this trip so we could sign off our ministry emails for the entire two weeks. A true respite from church work is rare, but our souls have responded with such gratitude. We head home in two days, and it is only now—ten days into the trip—that I am beginning to feel like I can go back to church fresh, and not on the edge of burnout. I've seen the spring begin to return to Daryl's step as well. The grace of an annual extended Sabbath is one we are learning to accept for the sake of both our ministry and our souls.

Today while the boys napped, Daryl and I curled up together. We talked about lessons from this pilgrimage we wanted to hold on to when we landed back in the hubbub of reality—ministry and school and appointments and household chores and grocery runs and crises of various degrees. Lessons of slowness, of stepping back from the digital world, of finding time to rest and read and play, of giving our kids our full attention rather than peering at them from behind a screen.

I'm nearly ready for the ordinary everyday again, to be in the comfort of my own kitchen and bed, the convenience of my own closet and pantry. I'm beginning to feel pangs of both homesickness and the sadness of leaving family, many of whom we won't see for an entire year or more. The bittersweetness itself is a good sign; it means we've drunk deeply of the opportunity for respite, but it also means we're ready to go home.

Thank you, Jesus.

DAY 23: THE RETURN

Pilgrimage reminds us that the journey, provision, and destination are always God's. Always, despite our uncanny abilities to convince ourselves we're in control. The daily invitation is always, "Follow!" There's profound freedom there. We are not the captains of our souls, the masters of our fate, the drivers of the car. God leads; we need only follow, receive, go, obey.

As we loaded up the car today, the kids were in tears. Leaving cousins and aunts and uncles and grandparents and an all-you-can-eat buffet with daily French toast and smiley-face potatoes is hard indeed. I blinked, holding back my own tears, wondering acutely, as I do each year, if this would be the last time I saw my grandparents on this earth. We double-checked suitcases and backpacks and driver's licenses and snacks, buckled in, and waved a final goodbye. Two airplanes, three time zones, and eight states stood between us and our beds.

Today the call of God was clear—go home. We are ready to be back in our neighborhood, back at church, back among friends and congregants alike. I miss my kitchen. Linc misses his goldfish. Wilson misses his tricycle. Daryl misses grabbing his friends for a night of Ping-Pong.

As we pulled up to the airport for the first flight of a long day, I found myself humming an old Fernando Ortega song as my prayer, a prayer applicable not just today as our journey sends us home, but all the days of the pilgrimage of living as a follower of Jesus on the adventure of a lifetime: *Heavenly Father, remember the traveler. Bring us safely home. Safely home.*[100]

JOIN THE JOURNEY

Where will your next travels take you? Whether it's just down the road or across the world, reframe the journey as not just a trip but a pilgrimage—an opportunity to meet God along the way, at the destination; and then anew, with fresh eyes, once you return home. Pray before embarking on your pilgrimage, as you remember along the way, and once you arrive. Include your family in the prayers, and invite your significant other and kids to pray, too. Don't shy away from including even the youngest in your cadre— Wilson's only two years old, but even he loves to fold his hands and pray ("God...Mama...Daddy...LaLa [Lincoln]...Baby... Me") like his mom and dad and big brother.

Here are some Scriptures about the call to follow Jesus to help guide you on your way:

1 Kings 18
Jonah 1–2
Matthew 4:18–22
Mark 6:7–12
Acts 20:13–38

CHAPTER 11

CEASING & CELEBRATION
Discovering the Playful God

*It suddenly dawned on them that the wildest dreams
they'd ever had hadn't been wild enough.*
—Frederick Buechner

Odds are that if you're a parent, you're pretty well versed in self-denial. We regularly give up sleep, sacrifice financially, and offer up our time, words of comfort, boo-boo fixes, book-reading marathons, and sibling fight referee skills. We drive to every blessed game and recital and concert and sit in the stands pretending that a wandering herd of four-year-olds kicking a ball around or a ragtag bunch of preteens performing *Oliver* is absolutely riveting. Sacrifice is the name of the parenting game. I can't even remember when I ate the last blueberry, because blueberries are my kids' favorite, so I can't ever bear to eat the final handful from the communal bowl because someday they'll graduate and move away and there will no longer be chubby little arms to hug my neck every day and I'll be achingly sad. But also I'll eat the last blueberry. And sleep in with some regularity. (Okay, maybe I won't be *that* sad.)

For parents, putting ourselves second, or third, or last-by-a-mile is often just a natural result of raising kids. We give and give, and when our reservoirs run dry, we almost always find a way to give just a little bit more. Sure, we can and should and do find bits of time for ourselves here and there to guard against going absolutely bat-flapping bananas, but these are largely graces and gifts and exceptions. Par for the course is cooking dinner *again*. Folding laundry *again*. Stepping on those gosh-darned Legos in front of the kids without letting any profanity fly *again*. (Stars in our heavenly crowns, friends. Stars in our crowns.)

The majority of spiritual practices, from fasting to stillness to servanthood, naturally fall somewhere on the spectrum of self-denial. And not without reason—it was Jesus himself who said, "Whoever wants to be my disciple must deny themselves and take up their cross and follow me."[101] There is wisdom to be gained in self-sacrifice, strength in surrender, and peace in submission to the one who gives us life. In giving up lesser things, we gain true and lasting treasure.

Yet God is not simply a God of rules and regulations, of to-do lists to complete and spiritual marathons to run. God is also the God of *joy*. Jesus turned water into wine—*good* wine—after all, not because doing so upheld an ancient religious law, but because eating and drinking and being merry was part and parcel of celebrating a wedding. Cardinal John Henry Newman once wrote of the feast of Christmas that "it is good to be joyful—it is wrong to be otherwise."[102] In the Psalms, in the Incarnation, in the vivid metaphors of Revelation, God bursts forth with jubilation. Certainly there will be times God calls us to austerity, but not all the time. Never always. There are regular, repeated times at which God invites us, even *implores* us, to celebrate.

CELEBRATION

MARKING PLEASURE WITH AN ENJOYABLE
PRACTICE—A PARTY, FESTIVAL, FOOD, DRINK,
OR OTHER COMMEMORATION. WHILE CELEBRATION
OFTEN INVOLVES A SOCIAL ELEMENT—
INVITING OTHERS TO JOIN IN OUR FESTIVITIES—
IT MAY ALSO BE PRACTICED ALONE.

Of all the spiritual disciplines, celebration may be the one that comes hardest to me. My mom lives for celebrations—she crafted themed birthday parties for my sisters and me until we were well into our teens, invites small villages of people over for cookouts, and makes sure a surprise dessert arrives at the restaurant table when there is any milestone to speak of. Me? I take after my dad, who used to look across our dining room table at an elaborate centerpiece my mom painstakingly crafted from flowers she'd grown herself—fighting off a small herd of white-tailed deer that treated her garden like a salad bar—and say, "Can we move the shrubbery? I can't see."

I long for my mother's deep appreciation for celebration, but if a propensity for joyful abandon is genetic, then in this particular area I'm all Dad. It isn't that he doesn't enjoy life; it's just that he'd rather go to bed early than visit another museum, even if we did fly all the way to Paris. I married someone of similar ilk; Daryl and I don't really *do* a lot of the regularly scheduled celebrations that dot the American calendar. On Valentine's Day, Mother's Day, and Father's Day, at some point we look at one another and say, "Happy holiday!" I send my mom and dad cards, of course—I'm not an *animal*—but that's the extent of it. A few months ago Daryl called me from the mall and asked if he could buy the newest Apple gadget for his birthday.

"It's April," I said. "Your birthday is in July."

"Believe it or not, I know that," he said. "But now you don't have to buy me a present later."

"Sweet."

It isn't that we don't ever feel happy—we do, and regularly. It's that enacted celebrations take time and work and cost money, and our notoriously tight budget and trimmed calendar tend to leave us most content when we simply don't celebrate, at least not lavishly. We throw modest birthday parties for the kids; we dole out lots of hugs and milkshake runs for school milestones; I make pancakes in crowd-pleasing shapes on special occasions; but other than that, we soft-pedal celebration. Yet the more I read and studied the Scriptures, the more I realized this wasn't the virtue I'd thought it to be. In fact, it might even be a vice.

GOD OF JOY

God doesn't just give us permission to celebrate; he practically commands it. There are seven prescribed festivals in the Hebrew Bible, from the Passover, commemorating God's sparing of Israel's firstborn, to the Festival of Firstfruits, a day to remember God's provision at the start of the harvest season. In addition to these, there were five major banquets, a monthly New Moon feast, and a weekly Sabbath celebration. Each of these festivals included times of rest, partying—good food and good wine were *big* in the Bible—and giving thanks to God. Every single one of these celebrations forced participants to take time away from the daily grind, all the things that *needed* to be done, in order to perform acts of commemoration and delight that turned God's people back to him in praise. Even in trying Old Testament times, celebration helped make life worth living. Who has time to celebrate? None of us, really. Which is why we *must*.

It can be incredibly sweet to think back on moments of celebration. I remember looking out over a sea of friends and family who'd traveled to northern Wisconsin in January for our wedding over a decade ago and dancing to oldies with my bridesmaids, my husband of mere hours standing with tears in his eyes. There was the night Daryl and I finished an arduous interview weekend and celebrated surviving it at a fancy beachside restaurant, dreaming about a possible future at a church in California, prayerfully offering our hopes to God over the best piece of fish I've ever eaten. I celebrated signing my first book contract in that California church's copy room and then took a dorky selfie because I knew I'd want to remember that moment forever, messy topknot, sloppy sweater, and all.

I thought of Daryl's PhD graduation—the one we almost didn't attend in person because schlepping young kids across the country is no small feat. A couple months before the ceremony his dad called us and said, "You're going, right? You *have* to go." We dutifully bought tickets and booked a rental car. When Daryl walked across that stage in his saffron robe and silly hat, announced for the first time as Rev. Dr. Ellis, my heart nearly burst.

My parents and grandparents flew out to be there, too—in part to help us with the kids, but mainly because we don't have any PhDs in our immediate family, so this was a big deal. My mom held squirmy one-year-old Wilson through the outdoor ceremony until he fell asleep in her arms; my dad took the video. When the ceremony ended, the administration invited everyone into two celebratory tents, one filled with flutes of champagne, the other with mountains of fresh strawberries, powdered sugar, and chocolate medallions.

"The strawberries are this way," my mom said, noticing my beeline for the bubbly. I don't drink much, vastly preferring sweets and starches to cocktails and wine.

"Yes," I told her, not changing course. "I know." It had taken Daryl seven long years of struggle and study and sacrifice, much of which—the time, the tension, the flights to and fro—we bore together as a family. You'd better bet I was going to drink some free champagne.

I thought of a staff meeting at church where we'd all been invited to share how we'd seen God at work in our ministries. After each person spoke—our children's director, youth pastors, head of staff, administrative assistants—we wrote their praises on a giant sheet of paper to hang in the break room and blew party horns. That "share and celebrate" meeting was years ago, but our senior pastor still has a party horn taped atop his computer monitor as a reminder to celebrate the good work of God and the church.

Celebration reminds us of who we are and whose we are, anchoring us to the truth that God is at work in our midst. Joyful remembrance frees us from our mundane routines, helping us to see our lives, our neighbors, our families, and our circumstances in a new light. Celebration is an essential spiritual practice, but in the busyness of keeping a young family moving forward, it's too easily forgotten. Sure, we throw birthday bashes, spend too much money at Christmastime, and dabble in sugar highs at Easter; but beyond that, there is little regular celebration. I'm not alone in my practical Grinch-dom. It is almost always easier *not* to celebrate. That is one of the reasons we must.

THE JOURNEY BEGINS

For this month's experiment, I would periodically cease my everyday activities—the daily grind, the striving, the church work, even the writing—to practice celebration in two ways:

1) **I would go to the beach twice a week, every week, no matter what.** I could do whatever I desired once I got there—eat a popsicle, stare at the seagulls, take a nap, turn right around and drive home—but I had to go.

2) **Our family would throw a summer barbecue at our house,** inviting friends and neighbors to an open house as a celebration of God's goodness to us and our love for them.

DAY 1: WE ALL HAVE TO START SOMEWHERE

Daryl and I chose a date for the barbecue, and I began immediately hyperventilating.

"Celebration is supposed to be fun," he reminded me.

"I'm an introvert," I reminded him—unnecessarily, since we'd just run into three acquaintances while out at the supermarket and, after the initial pleasantries, I disappeared into the vitamin section until they headed to the checkout line. The part of grocery shopping where you run into someone you know and make lovely small talk and everything is fine, but then you run into them *seven more times* in the same store…it practically kills me with its awkwardness.

"Celebration is sometimes supposed to involve other people," he reminded me. "Also, this was *your* idea."

"I know. I'm *working* on it."

DAY 2: A COAST GUARD CELEBRATION

My childhood friend Ian is a senior chief petty officer in the Coast Guard. For the past couple of years, he's been stationed near us in Long Beach, he and his wife and their daughter thrilling at the California weather, the breaking waves, the breezy winds, and the mosquitoless nights like only a family raised in the northern Midwest can. He and I grew up sitting around bonfires together, his siblings and my sisters and the two of us a tight-knit crew of outdoorsy, adventurous, constantly barefoot kids. He's spent the last two years in charge of a huge swath of coastline, from Dana Point in south Orange County to Morro Bay up north of Pismo Beach. Seeing him in uniform, dress blues bedecked with badges and ribbons and insignia, so official and solemn and distinguished, makes me feel a little bit like he's playing dress-up.

"His parents can't make it out this week," his wife, Amy, told us. "Plus you guys are basically our West Coast family. Will you come?"

It's not often an old friend is honored in such a significant way, so I'm up in Long Beach on the Coast Guard base to witness his change in command ceremony as he hands over authority of the post to another officer and leaves for his next assignment in the Midwest. I sit with Amy and their daughter, Alivia, on folding chairs spread across a bright green lawn that runs up against a calm blue sea, surrounded by officers and enlisted men and women, officials and dignitaries and friends. Mid-ceremony, a flashy orange helicopter zooms overhead, nearly clipping the tallest palm tree. Ships motor in and out of the harbor as the officers speak, a chaplain prays, and the national anthem sounds from an amplifier hidden behind the platform.

During Ian's speech, his voice suddenly breaks as he describes the support of his community during the past year when his daughter, just five years old, was diagnosed with cancer. Today those gathered celebrate not only Ian's change of command but Alivia's end of chemotherapy and her recent cancer-free scan. She wears a sunbonnet—her hair just beginning to grow back—a pink dress, and a wide smile. As soon as the ceremony ends, she rolls around on the lawn with a few preschool friends, each of them giggling and squinting into the sun. Amy stands looking relieved and proud and strong and remarkably tranquil for someone who is getting on a plane to move two thousand miles away in fewer than twenty hours. And for a mom whose daughter was only proclaimed cancer-free a few weeks earlier. I don't know how she's done it.

Afterward we all take pictures and shake hands and hug. Then there are tacos and *horchata*. The Coast Guard knows how to celebrate.

DAY 3: EVEN CONFLICT IS BETTER AT THE BEACH

It's date night for Daryl and me. The first one in over a month. After a day of playing with the kids and attending to nagging house jobs, Daryl and I clean ourselves up, tell the sitter where to find the fish sticks, and drive to a beachside restaurant just in time for happy hour. Happy hour is the only secret I know to affordable date nights in California. We eat five-dollar chicken kebabs at a cute little Mediterranean bistro and splurge on a seven-dollar hummus plate. (It *is* date night, after all.) If we lean a certain way at our outdoor table, we can just glimpse the Pacific. The weather is perfect in that way California gets right more often than seems fair—warm, but not hot, with a slight breeze. Not an insect in sight. I breathe it all in.

After dinner, we walk the beach. It's filled with families, kids chasing waves, aggressive seagulls, teenage couples lying on sandy blankets, older folks waiting with big cameras for the sun to set.

Daryl and I haven't seen each other much during the past week, and we've managed our way through a few marital squabbles by texting, so I'm expecting this date won't be all wine and roses. Sure enough, I'm right.

"Is there anything you need to talk about?" he asks me, which is Daryl-code for "*I* have something I want to talk about," because I'm the conflict-averse one in our relationship, and he's the human bulldozer.

"Nope," I say, sitting down in a dry patch of sand, "but it sounds like you do."

Bit by bit he lays out his simmering frustrations: home disorganization, inconsistency in chores, the chaos of an average work morning. I listen; I nod; I agree with most things and push back on a few. Often it isn't until we're engaged in a disagreement that I find words to put to my own irritations, and he listens to me in turn: how it can be frustrating to live with someone whose expectation is perfection, how a certain comfort with some level of bedlam is a necessary skill to develop when living with young kids, how being angry about the entropy isn't productive. He smooths out the sand beside him with his palms; I toss pebbles down the beach. He presses me; I push back. So much of the dance of marriage is learning to listen without defensiveness; to speak truth with gentle firmness; to follow a tiff all the way to its end; to admit and confess sins and shortcomings; to forgive, to forgive, to forgive. No one tells you when you walk starry-eyed down the aisle that marriage will be such a school for holiness and humility.

Somehow, between two high schoolers making out on a blanket to the thumping beat of Kendrick Lamar and a group of pale tourists climbing out on rocks far too slippery to be climbing out on, Daryl and I find one another again.

"I'm sorry," I say. "For how I've frustrated you. For the ways I haven't seen you. For the times I've let things slide, knowing you'd pick up the slack."

"I'm sorry, too," he says. "For the ways you've served our family that I haven't noticed or acknowledged. For how I sometimes hold everyone to an impossible and unhealthy standard. For the ways you've felt unseen."

He reaches for my hand, but I'm not quite ready to be affectionate yet. I need another minute of walking, of sand, of the dependability of the waves rushing up and back unceasingly. There is hope in this great blue metaphor of ocean: the hope that even in its most exhausting moments, marriage is worth its work. Ebb and flow. Love and conflict. Honesty and listening. Sometimes celebration looks less like joy and more like the ceasefire after a great friction, when everyone is a little tired and worn, but thankful nonetheless for the progress, for moving forward. Small celebrations count, too.

We brush the sand from our feet and walk back up to the main street, where we stumble upon a little French bakery selling macarons.

"These will help," I tell Daryl. He reaches for my hand, and this time I give it.

DAY 7: CELEBRATION SHOULD BE FUN, RIGHT?

When I read ancient history, I'm always amazed at how much war there is. I mean, weren't people just trying to *survive*? When half of infants didn't make it to their first birthday and heinous diseases like cholera and dysentery ran rampant, why not just say, "Hey—we don't have much time left to live anyway. What say we go figure out farming irrigation and work to eradicate the plague, and just be nice to each other?" Who had time to make war when they had so little time to begin with?

Speaking of which, I can already tell that I absolutely will not have time to go to the beach this week. We live twenty minutes from the Pacific—a fact that still feels like a small miracle four years after our move from the Midwest—but I almost never go. Going twice last week was delightful, but a total fluke.

"It's too far away," I tell myself. "By the time I've driven and parked, it's half an hour, and who has that much time to waste celebrating?"

But here's the thing—it's the *ocean*. Who doesn't love the ocean? My friends and family members who live landlocked regularly chew me out for not taking advantage of my front-row seat to its salty allure. For less gas money than it takes me to drive the kids to the nearest petting zoo, I can watch waters roll in that once lapped the shores of Japan and Hawaii and Alaska. I can feel the sand beneath my toes and the wind on my face and watch sand pipers doing their hippity hoppity sand piper thing up and down in the waves. But I don't do any of this, because who has time? There is laundry to fold and emails to send, the kids need dinner, and I need to collapse in an armchair in front of Twitter. Because *that* I have time for.

Yet it seems like every Scripture I read lately reminds me of the biblical invitation to celebrate. The Psalms are chock-full of proclamations of the goodness of God. Matthew chronicles the many festivals Jesus and his family attended. Even Leviticus—often viewed as the wet blanket of the Old Testament—devotes chapter upon chapter to the importance of celebration, with God telling Moses, "Speak to the Israelites and say to them: 'These are my appointed festivals, the appointed festivals of the Lord, which you are to proclaim as sacred assemblies.'"[103]

It goes on from there to mention the Sabbath, the Passover, the Festival of Unleavened Bread, the Offering of Firstfruits, the Festivals of Weeks, Trumpets, and Tabernacles, and the Day of Atonement. Each milestone, every season of life, was marked by celebration—partying, pageantry, praise. The daily grind didn't anchor the annual calendar; the soirées did.

So I guess tomorrow I'll haul myself to the beach, even though I need to do the grocery shopping and my sermon for this upcoming Sunday is a legit mess. In light of all I have to do for my family and my congregation, celebration seems...selfish. Unnecessary. A luxury I can do without. Yet God commands it, so here I am.

Why am I resisting this so?

DAY 8: A LITTLE CHILD SHALL LEAD THEM

My oldest son turns six in three months. Well, to be technical about it, he turns six in seventy-nine days. I know for sure because he's counting. He's carefully selected a list of friends to invite; he's chosen a theme (half *Cars 3*, half pirate...good luck to us on that one); he's put in his request for a vanilla cake with blueberry icing and rainbow sprinkles. Kids? *They* know how to celebrate.

But I don't. I really, really don't. There is so much to do, so much suffering in the world; there are so many other things to save money for; I just can't shake the thought that celebration is wasteful. Excessive. Needless. What if the washing machine conks out next week, and we can't afford to replace it because we threw a totally unnecessary barbecue? Daryl has worked ridiculously long days this week—how can I ask him to watch the kids for another hour just so I can dip my toes in the waves? (I realize I could take the kids with me to the ocean, but bringing a five-year-old who is *certain* he can swim to a riptide-laden coast and a two-year-old who wants to be held constantly while I'm already carrying his uncomfortably large little sister in my womb is less a celebration than an exercise in exhaustion.)

My Protestant work ethic runs deeper than I first realized. I come from a family of *doers*, a church of *doers*. Our identity exists largely in what we accomplish—for our families, our bank accounts, our God. At the end of the day, I won't net any profits from my beach walks in a tangible sense. So why even go?

Maybe I'll go tomorrow instead.

DAY 10: IN WHICH I ADMIT TO BEING A BAD PERSON

Can I share a little secret with you? I hate kid birthday parties. I really, really hate them. I can handle my own kids' parties—those don't bug me as much, because I have a clear job description and can stay busy cutting the cake, directing kid traffic, running games, handing out pointy hats. But I struggle with other kids' parties so much that I tend to come home ranting about how much I hate them, so Daryl finally asked if he could take over the kid birthday party circuit and I could stay home and do something—anything—else.

"What if I clean the house while you guys are at the party?" I asked.

"Done," he said.

Birthday parties feel like a weird sort of trap to me. As Oscar Martinez says in *The Office*, "You go, and there's really nothing for you to do there, but the kid's having a really good time so you're kinda *there*."[104] It isn't that I don't love kids—I do. It's the small talk that gets to me. Making small talk about the weather—which, by the way, in California is limited to gorgeous and seventy-five degrees or *literally* on fire—with dozens of people I will almost certainly never, ever see again is torture. I'd literally rather scrub toilets.

I didn't go the beach today. But I did scrub a couple of toilets.

DAY 12: YOU GUYS, THE BEACH IS BEA-U-TI-FUL

It was our family Sabbath today, and Lincoln's been begging for a beach trip, so we all went together. Getting two children ready to go to the beach is like doomsday prepping. For ourselves, Daryl and I each bring a water bottle, sunglasses, and a granola bar. We wear our swimsuits and don't mind riding home with soggy behinds. But the kids? They each require enough provisions to survive a nuclear holocaust. Clothes, towels, floaties, food, hats, sunscreen, water, more food, more water. How many buckets and shovels do they actually *need*? All of them. And a few from the neighbor's garage, just in case.

As soon as we parked at the beach, Lincoln shot out of the car, running down the sand, kicking up his heels like a fawn in spring. No one needs to teach him to celebrate. Wilson was nursing a cold and feeling clingy, riding my hip like a little blond koala bear, content to sit on my lap and draw patterns in the sand with his shovel. Since we work Sundays, Daryl and I take our Fridays off as a family day dedicated to God, a sacred Sabbath. We need it desperately and are thankful beyond reason for it every week, though we've learned to expect we will nearly always arrive at it cranky and out of sorts as the stresses of the week crash down around our heads.

"You okay?" I asked, squeezing Daryl's knee from our perch in a little pop-up sun shelter—another thing the kids apparently require.

He wasn't, not really. There were financial fears on his mind; worries about the house; stresses about emails not yet sent and meetings not yet scheduled. Exhaustion plagued him. It was all he could do to pack up and get us down to the beach.

I was fighting my own demons: behind in a writing project, the sickly sharp claws of pregnancy nausea not yet fully released from my gut. I'd stayed up too late the night before—one of the downsides to signing off of all technology for our family Sabbath is that Daryl and I inevitably stay up too late the night before, reading the news, checking in on all the social media, putting off the rest God grants us as long as possible. Much like celebration, rest is hard.

We sat together in silence, watching the waves and the boys, here to celebrate even though we weren't really feeling it. I figure that I need to at least be willing to accept God's invitation to celebration in the same spirit I've begun to submit to his other calls in Scripture. If I'm willing to fast and contemplate and serve and even suffer in stillness, surely I can celebrate. And if I won't do it willingly, at least I can give it a try out of obligation, right? Celebration as duty! Leave it to me to ruin a good party with moral imperatives. My Puritan ancestors would be proud.

The longer we sat in silence, the harder it became not to feel at least a *little bit* celebratory with a big, blue ocean rolling up and down and a pudgy toddler blissfully pushing a tiny dump truck around our feet. God even threw in a couple of dolphins for good measure, and a lifeguard who let Lincoln climb the guard tower and use a spare pair of binoculars for a few moments.

"I guarded the *whole* beach," Linc told us, his little chest puffed out with pride.

In the face of such vast beauty—the breezy blue yonder, a kind lifeguard, two boys enjoying God's goodness in their own ways, the Sabbath rest God gave—even I had to take a few deep breaths and simply enjoy.

DAY 14: SO BIG, SO STRONG, SO GOOD

I went to the beach again today. I had to, or I'd flunk this week, since it's Day 14 already. I took my laptop to a beachside coffee shop, drinking an orange juice—Baby #3 gifts me with raging heartburn after even a sip of coffee—enjoying the salty breeze. From where I sat, the ocean rose up before me into low-hanging clouds, blurring where one ended and the other began.

The immensity of the ocean continually surprises me. I grew up on the shores of a little Wisconsin lake that, to me as a young girl, looked plenty big and wild. When the northern winds blew down from Canada with all the force of the coming winter behind them, the waves would whip up into whitecaps. In the spring, when the thaw came, the thick surface ice would crack and groan like a waking monster. Yet the ocean is on another scale altogether, so enormous as to be nearly incomprehensible.

Sitting so close to such magnificence might even make a person think about God.

DAY 17: DEADLY SERIOUSNESS CAN BE PRETTY DEADLY

For any of you into the Enneagram, I'm a Type 2 and Daryl is a Type 1. This means, among other things, we are very earnest people who believe that we can, if we try with all our might, work hard enough to save ourselves and also the entire world. Daryl's a reformer, a truth-speaker, no-nonsense when it comes to faith and holiness. He's forever trying to design perfect systems, both at church and at home, that will save us from entropy. I'm a helper, a feeler, invested in close relationships and deep conversations and authenticity. He experiences the impulse to improve everything all the time, and I wrestle with deep, constant grief over the state of the world. Put simply: we are easily much too serious much of the time.

A few years ago the band Sleeping at Last put out songs for each of the Enneagram types, and "One" begins, "Now hold on for a minute, 'cause I believe that we can fix this…"[105] That pretty much sums it up.

I'm sure someone, somewhere has written about what happens when an Enneagram Type 1 and a Type 2 try to throw a party. If not, I'll do it here:

They don't.

Parties seem almost unbearably frivolous in light of all the work there is to be done. But God does not major in seriousness. God is just and wise, yes. Bonhoeffer once described him as "entirely in earnest."[106] But God is also the one who created every single person with a unique laugh; giraffes with seven-inch-long purple tongues; a wide, wild universe studded with stars and planets and nebulas and black holes. God invites us to join him in the afterlife not for harp playing and good-deed-doing, but for a lavish wedding feast in a shining city with a bold river running down its center. "Blessed are those who are invited to the marriage supper of the Lamb," John writes in Revelation.[107]

Yet somewhere deep inside I believe it is inherently more spiritual to spend money on toothpaste and oil changes than party hats and popsicles.

I don't know why, but I really do.

DAY 20: LIKE A CHILD, OR MAYBE A COLLEGE STUDENT

I help lead our church's college and young adults group, and this weekend is our annual summer camping trip. We pitch tents a quarter mile from the beach; one of the dads cooks pancakes and burgers; we roast s'mores around a fire. The college students are back in town for a few months, each looking a bit taller in mental stature. There are new goatees, piercings, romances. No one is as enthusiastic on this trip as our newly minted high school graduates, initiated into the group as full-fledged adults, even though a few of the guys still can't grow facial hair. On Sunday morning we will celebrate Communion together on the beach, gathering around the Lord's Table to remember his body, broken for us, and his blood, shed for us.

Today was the first day of the trip, so everyone was a little nervous. They signed up for this weekend, for this retreat, but familiar faces are now a little bit unfamiliar after months away at Berkeley or Westmont or UCLA. Still, most young adults have yet to lose their love for celebration. Much of it comes out in random goofiness. Last year one of them wore an Angels baseball cap for three days straight; another set up a slackline (a thin strip of fabric webbing used for tightrope walking) over jagged rocks, promising me everyone would be okay in the end, but giving me several near-heart attacks in the interim. One girl brought *Paradise Lost* to the beach when everyone else was elbow-deep in Doritos—truly a reader after my own heart. A tall, lanky guy ignored the tents completely, instead setting up a queen-sized mattress in the bed of his truck.

I love these young adults, their authenticity, their humor, their love of memes far beyond my understanding. The depth of their faith encourages and astounds me. I love their love for one another and the church—many of them have walked through the fire in the past few years, learning that Jesus was there all the while. When the sun sets, we sit around the campfire and sing his praises.

Left to my own devices, I wouldn't go on this camping trip at all. I'm an introvert. (A pregnant introvert.) Weekends are for sleeping, for hanging with my kids, for reading as many books as I am physically able. Yet these annual weekends have become life-changing for me, too. I inevitably come home filled with new hope, a deeper understanding of the mysteries of the faith, of what it means to pass it on to a new generation, to watch it take a new form. I'm grateful for retreats that draw me out of my hermitage and into the wider stream of Christian community. As Ruth Haley Barton writes, "This is fundamentally what spiritual transformation is all about: choosing a way of life that opens us to the presence of God in the places of our being where our truest desires and deepest longings stir."[108] This weekend I celebrate what God is doing in their midst, and what he's doing within me, too.

DAY 22: CHRIST HAS DIED, CHRIST IS RISEN, CHRIST WILL COME AGAIN

Last year a visiting pastor celebrated Communion with us at the campsite. Steve, fifteen years my senior with grown kids of his own, encouraged me to bring Lincoln along. "Your kids need to see your vocation," he said. "Let them watch you loving Jesus whenever you can."

Lincoln was then only four and a half years old, and I brought him along with fear and trembling, wondering if I'd be able to get anything done with a rambunctious little boy at my heels. He spent the morning digging holes in the dirt, poking the ashes of the fire with a stick, and bumming candy off of the college students. They folded him in like one of their own, and he practically glowed with pride. He behaved quite well, despite my misgivings, but I would have sworn he retained nothing from our morning but a carb-and-sugar high and a bit of sun.

Yet after we packed everything up and arrived home, he pulled down his children's Bible from the shelf and turned to the story of the Last Supper.

"Mommy, this is what Pastor Steve was talking about," he said earnestly. "This is what it means to be a disciple of Jesus." He paused, furrowing his brow. "Mommy, were the big kids at the camp disciples of Jesus?" I answered yes, they were. "Mommy, are *you* a disciple of Jesus?" I answered in the affirmative again, and he pondered this. "Can I be one, too?"

Oh God, I thought to myself, not blasphemously, but in an honest prayer. *Oh God, this is happening right now. Help me not to mess it up too badly.* I always assumed my theologian husband would be the one to guide Lincoln across the threshold of this decision. I'm a trained pastor with years of Greek and Hebrew and seminary under my belt, but he's the one with a deeper understanding of the nuances of the language of God. Yet here I was, my preschool son earnestly asking if he could give his life to Jesus, my husband out running errands. It looked as if the storytelling parent and not the PhD was God's choice for this momentous event.

"Of course!" I said. We talked a bit more, sitting together on the ancient sand-colored carpet of our tiny rented condo, him snuggled into the crook of my arm, his tousled hair even blonder from our morning in the sun; and then we prayed. Heaven reached down to earth right there on the floor of Lincoln's bedroom as my firstborn asked Jesus to make him his disciple. The depth and profundity gripped my soul; but it was a surprisingly ordinary moment, too, as natural to Lincoln as asking if he could go to the park in the morning or have another pancake at breakfast. Jesus had been calling to him for a long time; in many ways, the two of them were already well acquainted.

This year Lincoln came back with me to the campground for Sunday worship. I was the celebrant today, preaching and praying and passing out the bread and juice. *Body of Christ, broken for you. Blood of Christ, shed for you.* We passed the elements around our little circle, offering them to each other: first the bread, then the juice. I handed them to Lincoln, my firstborn several inches taller than last year, his formerly white-blond hair darkening to sandy brown, his once baby-round face thinning out into boyhood, his palms upturned and outstretched, waiting for the bread and the cup.

"Body of Christ," I said. "For you. For you."

That which Daryl and I had prayed for since before Lincoln was even conceived came to fruition because of the witnesses to faith—a pastor, a dozen or so college students—at this same campground a year ago. In the time between last year's celebration of the Lord's Supper and this one, Lincoln chose Jesus again and again. The college students who gathered here this weekend, the working twenty-somethings, my co-leader and I: we are all responding and learning to better respond to God's plain and persistent call. This morning we celebrated Christ's body, broken for us, gathered in a circle of people making up the body of Christ.

Faith is a journey, of course. Praying a single prayer is not magic; Lincoln will be faced with the decision of whether or not to follow God a thousand more times over the course of his life. Yet we all begin somewhere, with a decision that sets us on a path.

I ponder this holy mystery, celebrating again that my firstborn is a disciple of Jesus, celebrating the Lord's Supper with him at a dusty campsite, celebrating the earnest faces around the circle of those young and old seeking to follow Jesus in the same way. The celebration of the kingdom is right here in our midst; it practically brings me to my knees with tears of joy and thanksgiving.

We closed in prayer, and our circle broke, and Lincoln jumped up and called out, "Okay, who wants to play Frisbee?"

DAY 28: WHEN CELEBRATION FEELS (OR IS) IMPOSSIBLE

A routine dental appointment today became decidedly less routine with the introduction of words like "root canal" and "massive infection" and "possible risk to your baby." My plan to leave the medical plaza and spend a half hour at the shore before heading off to evening worship dashed, I sat in my hot car in the parking lot, dialed Daryl, and promptly burst into tears.

"We will get you through this," he said. It wasn't the root canal that did me in, not really. It was the blindside, the painful twist in a day that was otherwise all planned out, the monkey wrench at the end of a long week when I'd been banking on a little beach time to connect with Jesus and blow off steam. Well, it was that combined with years and years of dental trauma preceding this one crummy afternoon.

For whatever reason, my baby teeth didn't fall out when I was a kid, leading to a dozen dental appointments spread over years to have those teeth yanked out by a dentist who never properly explained what he was about to do to me. I might have been seven years old, but I certainly knew the difference between a "magic icicle" and a giant needle filled with lidocaine, even if he made me close my eyes and asked me to use my imagination. Kids aren't stupid, y'all.

My beach time thwarted, I wore my sunglasses into the pharmacy to pick up my pregnancy-safe antibiotics, and then to a 7-11 where I bought a massive Coke Slurpee to numb my pain and ruin my remaining teeth.

I'm sorry, Jesus, I prayed. *I wanted to celebrate today, but I just can't.*

When life gets serious and heavy, complicated or expensive, physically or emotionally or spiritually painful, keeping and honoring celebration can feel like trying to carry a backpack full of rocks up a mountain. Pain brings seriousness, even deadly seriousness, and even small experiences in suffering can derail us from celebrating as God intends.

Yet celebration is crucial to emotional and spiritual health. Edwin Friedman notes playfulness—one of the key components of celebration—is "an attribute…which is an ingredient in both intimacy and the ability to maintain distance." It connects us with one another while also helping us to remember who we are as individuals—distinct from both the crisis before us and from the people around us. He continues, "In an atmosphere where everything is dire, a vicious cycle develops as a loss of playfulness destroys perspective."[109] This is why the Christian practice of celebration is perhaps most crucial when we least *feel* like it.

I ran out of time for the beach today. Circumstances and my papier-mâché teeth upended my plans. And to be honest, sitting there in my hot car, my mouth aching, I wanted much more to ignore God than to praise him. The week was a long one, I was tired and run-down, and instead of a little time to connect with the Most High, I got a root canal with a side of prenatal anxiety to boot. There was not much to celebrate. Not really.

Still, the spiritual practice of celebration is not just about the external trappings of festivals and feasts. Those outward signs are a signal of a much deeper internal truth. We celebrate because God *is*. God is good; God is present; God is love; God is here. The beach might fill me with joy, help me feel more like celebrating, remind me of the vastness of God's power and peace; but a good dentist and quick treatment and ready access to affordable antibiotics are no less a sign of the care of God.

Today I stopped, dried my tears, and celebrated in the small way that I could, right there in my aging, paint-peeling Toyota Corolla, baking under a mighty California sun.

I don't feel like celebrating, Jesus, I said. *I had other plans for how this day should end. But thank you for being here, for seeing me through, for preventing the infection from spreading, for the invention of lidocaine, for sunglasses to hide my red, puffy eyes, and for your love—vast as the ocean, even on a day I don't make it to the shore to see for myself.*

I'd go to the beach tomorrow, but the root canal isn't over yet—apparently some doctors like to do them in phases?—and also a plague of locusts might find me first. So for now the Slurpee will have to do. A small, sugary celebration of God's goodness in a blue paper cup, thanks to Jesus and my local convenience store. Glory hallelujah.

DAY 30: GOD BLESS AMERICA

Daryl and I both had July 4th off. As stated at this chapter's beginning, my celebratory goal for this month—a culmination of a year's worth of spiritual practices, the pièce de résistance of these divine disciplines—was a big backyard barbecue, a gathering of friends and neighbors for no other reason than to celebrate the summer and one another and God at work in our midst. This was the goal. The plan. The hope.

It did not happen.

Long story short, our backyard wasn't party-ready. Not in the "Martha Stewart perfection" sense, but in the "it's so hot people might get heatstroke and die" sense. You see, our backyard shade structure is taking longer to build than we anticipated. It's our first big DIY project in this new house, both to save money and to get our hands dirty creating something we need in order to make our backyard usable. Situated on the top of a south-facing hill in direct sunlight, if the local temperature is eighty degrees Fahrenheit, our backyard is approximately 110 degrees. Without shade, it's like the surface of Venus back there. But it turns out that having one-half of the adults in our house throwing up in the bathroom and going to bed at 7 p.m. turns even normal household tasks into an uphill climb—never mind labor-intensive backyard renovation projects.

So today, instead of hosting a celebration, we attended one. A barbecue in a friend's backyard, a slip-and-slide set up for the kids, beautiful shade, and a festive table. All we were asked to contribute was bread and a fruit salad. The celebration simply *was*; we were invited to come and enjoy. To celebrate without striving. If this isn't a parable for the past year of learning to receive from God, I don't know what is. Over and again I try to muscle my way into the path of the Holy Spirit, and time after time God says, "I'm here. I've got this. I've got *you*. Just open your hands and your heart and receive from me."

It isn't that there is no work for us to do in the world; on the contrary, there is much to be done. The earth is on fire; our neighbors are in need; our families require nurture and sacrifice and care. Yet without the ministrations of God's spirit to ours, the work is in vain. As Paul writes in 1 Corinthians, "If I...do not have love, I am only a resounding gong or a clanging cymbal."[110]

The love he writes of isn't something we drum up on our own; it flows from the source.

Today as we sat around a backyard table, our boys soaked to the skin from the slip-and-slide, our conversation seasoned with years of trust built in the kind of friendship where no question is off-limits and no protective façade remains, I celebrated with the abandon of someone invited to a table she didn't set, to enjoy food she didn't shop for or prepare. A table of grace set by dear friends and by Jesus himself.

Turns out that God waits to meet me at every turn, even when some of those turns are unexpected. And who knows? The summer is still young, and our backyard shade is nearly finished. Perhaps we can host a celebratory barbecue of our own in the coming weeks. In a blaze of spiritual depth of which I didn't even know I was capable…I have come to believe it might even be fun.

JOIN THE JOURNEY

Choose a celebratory practice you can do regularly—at least once or twice a week for a month. It should be something out of your ordinary routine that brings you joy. It's okay if it costs a little bit of money—celebration often does. Perhaps you, like me, live close to a beautiful view—a forest preserve, a beach, a mountain, a garden—and can play in it a couple of times each week. Or maybe there are exquisite chocolates you could eat while reading a new novel from the library. Perhaps you celebrate best with a group of friends, and you need to commit to celebrating out on the town with them regularly this month. Invite God into your celebration, and then drink in the joy. Taste and see that the Lord is good.

Here are a few Scriptures that may help as you begin this spiritual practice:

Psalm 118:24
Psalm 150
Proverbs 31:25
Ecclesiastes 3:1–13
Isaiah 61:10–11
Luke 15:23
1 Corinthians 5:8

CHAPTER 12

ALMOST HOLY, FULLY LOVED
Where Do We Go from Here?

Good living entails good reflection. Having been interrupted
by Jesus, we carry our questions with us.
—Jonathan Wilson-Hartgrove

In my late teens, I spent a summer volunteering at a rustic camp in Jackson, Wyoming. As was my common practice between hitting puberty and getting married, I immediately developed a galloping crush on an older boy. When tall, dark-haired, blue-eyed Jonathan asked me if I'd like to go on a hike with him—just the two of us—I jumped at the chance.

"Let's go up to Lake of the Crags," he said. "It's a long hike, and over a mile and a half straight up in elevation, too."

"Sounds like a plan," I responded, with what I hoped was nonchalance beyond my years. I was not about to let a few potential blisters derail my plans of a lengthy and satisfying romance with he of the broad shoulders, sinewy forearms, and part-time construction job. I was about to turn eighteen, blissfully overjoyed to be free of my eagle-eyed parents for a summer; he was in his early twenties and owned a truck. If he'd told me our hike would involve a blood sacrifice to twenty thousand ticks and mosquitos, I would have considered it still.

We left before dawn, and only a half-mile down the trail I realized this was to be much more of a climb than a hike, the dusty, rocky trail rising steep as a ladder before us. As the miles wore on, the air began to thin, I'd eaten all my snacks, and my head pounded in the altitude. Despite preventative Band-Aids, my feet rapidly turned to pulpy stumps inside my still-too-new boots. Apparently "long hike" meant something different to him than it did to me, a girl whose family occasionally took three-mile nature hikes in the decidedly flat Wisconsin forest. Too concerned with appearing cool to ask when the torture would end, my desire to be on this hike fading with every step (by now I'd deduced that he wasn't even going to *hold my hand*), I glanced up through a sheen of sweat to see—glory be!—the trail ending only a hundred yards or so ahead.

"Is that it?" I gasped. "Are we there?"

Jon laughed, not unkindly. "No," he said. "That's just another little plateau where we can rest for a bit." One more little flat spot in the trail, enough to catch a breath before continuing on our climb.

So it was with Lake of the Crags. So it is with our spiritual lives.

As we take on spiritual practices, Jesus invites us to follow the trail laid out before us, together treading the pilgrim path, the same route of holiness traversed by all the sinner-saints who've come this way before. The climb isn't easy, but the company is steadfast. And, thank heavens, much more promising than Jonathan ever was.

The main thrust of spiritual disciplines is simply putting one foot in front of the other, following Jesus as he leads, trusting the Holy Spirit in the process. (Also, it never hurts to bring extra snacks.) We slowly ascend, trusting there is a beautiful vista up ahead, realizing step by step that it will take us a lifetime to reach it. Done befittingly and repeatedly, these practices will continue on until our end, affording us moments (or days, months, or even years) of rest and reward before we resume our climb once again. As Scott Cairns puts it, "The *way*—it now became clearer to me— was inevitably a slow one, with prayer and stillness becoming only slightly more apprehensible as you go."[111]

The graces of this year have been abundant. I haven't achieved parental sainthood, and I'm still nowhere near an expert on any of the practices laid out in this book. But over the course of the past months I have grown familiar with them in unexpected and heartening ways, and through them I have begun to know and trust the Lord more intimately and deeply and fully. These disciplines have begun to teach me to be still, to listen, to become aware of God at work around and within me—to become aware of *God*.

I've failed continually and spectacularly, both in my parenting and in my spiritual practices, but these failures have, in a way, offered the deepest lessons of all. God is there when I fall, when I fail, on the days I decide not to care, not to try. God is there when the laundry doesn't get folded, when suffering forces stillness, when even celebration feels like a chore. God is there in my kids' shining eyes and tight hugs *and* in their tantrums when they are overtired or struggling to find words for their big feelings or just plain being naughty. God is with me when my husband and I melt into bed together, when we can hardly stand to be in the same car as one another, when we speak the hardest words of all—"I'm sorry. I was wrong. I love you." God has always been there, present within my family, within the four walls of our house, the people of our church and community, the streets of our neighborhood; but it is practicing these disciplines that has helped me to see.

Each small step takes us a pace farther up the trail to where the air is clearer, the sun is brighter, and the view begins to come into focus. From higher up we can see a clearer picture of God—Father, Son, and Holy Spirit—and a less clouded view of our neighbors, too: our kids, our spouses, our communities. A more transparent picture of our own souls—tired, longing, faltering, loved.

Above all, I've begun to learn afresh that I cannot save myself or anyone else—only God can do that. Spiritual disciplines, at their heart, are not vain attempts at being a better person, a better mom, a better Christian, but practices of drawing closer to the God who offers renewal, rest, and rejoicing day by day. The God who refills our reservoirs so we can wake to a new day every day.

Saint Benedict composed a Rule of Life for those who sought to follow his spiritual practices: guidelines for living more faithfully, for turning to Jesus more regularly. At the end of this year, modern, parent-friendly practices like the Examen, showering with Scripture, and stepping off of social media for a time have begun to develop something of the same within me. While I can't pray at five fixed hours every day as St. Benedict advises, I am learning to look for Jesus in the laundry and the dishes, the car rides and the bedtime routines; for it is in these invitations that he reminds me he is there already. He has been there all along.

HOW DO YOU MEASURE SPIRITUAL GROWTH?

While this experiment irreversibly and profoundly changed my life, I am also still very much the same. Still an introvert; still someone who laughs too loudly at inopportune moments; still the spouse who sometimes chooses *The Office* over listening to my husband at the end of a long day; still a parent who has been known to hide in the pantry and eat the last of the M&M's so she doesn't have to share. But in exploring these spiritual disciplines with greater regularity, tying them to necessary parenting tasks, I've also felt my sharpest edges of impatience, selfishness, and anger begin to soften under the faithful sandpaper of the Holy Spirit. When a brutal first trimester shattered my pride, God met me in my forced stillness. When I showered with Scripture, God faithfully brought his words back to my mind in moments of fear, exhaustion, or frustration. When I entered into celebration, God surprised me with the depth of his love in how he celebrates us. I'm no longer the same, though there are infinite miles still to travel.

Spiritual disciplines are funny that way—they take lifetimes to reveal their full effects, but even a day of practicing them leaves us forever transformed. The paradox of the gospel is this ongoing dance—God is the primary performer, but we must play a part; God is the caller, and we give the response; God leads, and we can allow him to sweep us around the ballroom in joyful abandon, or choose to fight him every step of the way. Spiritual practices soften our hearts, open our eyes, attune our ears, and unclench our fists, working incrementally to heighten our awareness to God's presence, God's love, God's work. The disciplines are, as Thomas More once wrote, "to lean unto the comfort of God, busily to labour to love him."[112] They are also, as Elizabeth Barrett Browning once said, "gifts" that "put [humanity's] best dreams to shame."[113]

THE GIFT OF PARENTHOOD

In many ways, parenthood is as profound a preparation for these disciplines and as natural a place they can nest as any vocation under the sun. The ordinary rhythms of raising children are infused with God's presence and continual opportunity to pair spiritual practices with the mundane practicalities of parenting. Even more than my preparation for ministry—Christian college, seminary, internships, chaplaincies—nurturing my kids is teaching me that the work of faithfulness, of holiness, of intimacy is never complete. Every day we build on the foundation of days past, but we also begin anew. Every moment brings with it unique openings to love and be loved. The work of sanctification—growing into the people God created us to be—is never complete, but even this is grace. It is the unfinished nature of the labor that gives each hour its significance, its sweetness, its challenge, its reward.

Above all, communing more closely with Jesus these past few months has opened my eyes to the laboring mercies of parenthood. It is in the will-crushing monotony and back-breaking exhaustion of reading the same bedtime story for the tenth night in a row—of waking up for a midnight emergency after weeks of little sleep, of buying groceries and preparing a meal only to have it proclaimed "*So yuck*, Mom"—that the school of discipleship becomes real. Anyone can change a diaper, but sainthood beckons ever closer as we change another, and another, and another, finding that even in dealing with the smelliest mess there lies an opportunity to respond in love. As Douglas McKelvey writes in *Every Moment Holy:*

> Open my eyes that I might see
> this act for what it is
> from the fixed vantage of eternity, O Lord—

> how the changing of a diaper
> might sit upstream
> of the changing of a heart;
> how the changing of a heart
> might sit upstream
> of the changing of the world.[114]

Even with a growing understanding that parenthood's toughest moments are somehow blessings, too, my steps were (and are) halting at best. Yours will be, too. This is normal; bumbling advances are part of the long, slow journey of discipleship. The trail is long and often steep. Look at Peter, at Paul, at anyone in Scripture besides Jesus. Faltering steps, all.

Yet as we practice these spiritual tools, they shape us. Slowly and incrementally, but surely. Parenting, taken on without God's help, can be overwhelming in its monotony and chaos and exhaustion. But spiritual practices are an ordered way to awaken us to the fact that *in the midst* of these hardships, there is a parallel adventure of God growing us as we embrace his love and lessons. There's no training in discipleship like choosing love, again and again, in the crucible of parenting. It's not only a tremendous adventure; it's a life of incredible significance. Day in and day out, your children have the opportunity to learn from God, through you, that he is present in the day-to-dayness of life.

Is it easy? Nowhere near. Does it get any less demanding? I wish I could promise this, but my friends with older children assure me that the challenges never disappear; they just change as our children grow. But just as an athlete's trips to the weight room build muscle almost imperceptibly at first, so we are changed by showing up to meet with God. We never arrive, yet we slowly transform more and more into the people God created us to be. The loud-mouthed Peter we meet early in the gospels later brings

242   ALMOST HOLY MAMA

the good news of Jesus to the gentiles. Tradition teaches that
he is later martyred, crucified upside down because he considers
himself unworthy to die in the same way Jesus did upon the
cross. It's not something a bombastic man with shallow roots
would choose. Peter had grown up in Christ. We are invited to do
the same.

God splashed his grace all over this year's experiment, helping
me to notice things I'd otherwise have missed, meeting me in the
ups and the downs, and even preparing me for difficult seasons
I didn't know awaited me just ahead. Without the practices
of contemplation and the Examen, the first five months of
pregnancy with baby #3 would have felt much more severe.

God is good, friends. I have no doubt that he will meet you
in these practices, too.

A GUIDE THROUGH THE WILDERNESS

Seeking to become a holier mama is tough; raising kids brings
me to my knees more times than I can count. Yet herein I've
found one more mercy, and I offer this encouragement to you
in closing. Embracing spiritual practices as a parent is one way
of embracing God's profound affirmation of your parenting.
So much of mothering and fathering feels like anonymous
sacrifice—indeed, this is why the temptation to delegate it to
other people, to distract ourselves from it, or even not to have
children at all can be so very strong. But God's arrangement of
parenting for our own growth and goodness, and for the growth
and goodness of our beloved children, is a profound reminder
that parenting is never anonymous to God. In fact, a spiritual
parent is exactly what he is to us—we are his children.

So much of parenting is lonely—no one sees us rock our
babies back to sleep for the fourth time in a single night, pleading

for the dawn to hold off until we can get just an hour or two of sleep. Rarely is the laundry appreciated or the dinner praised. We receive no standing ovation for keeping an accident-prone toddler from toppling off the see-saw or gently correcting a saucy five-year-old for the hundredth time. Often no one sees these moments. No one but Jesus, that is.

As I stepped into the last few spiritual practices of this year's experiment—stillness, gratitude, pilgrimage, celebration—I began to see them less as things I *did* and more as opportunities to meet with Jesus, to let him fill me back up when my spiritual gas tank was empty. To enter in, drink deeply, show up and quiet my heart, waiting with expectation for the wild, windy Spirit to blow afresh over my stagnant, weary soul. Spiritual practices protect us from one of life's greatest tragedies—living the daily grind as if God wasn't there. Our whole lives are an invitation to walk with him; these disciplines open up space to embrace that fact, to overcome our own forgetfulness again and again, with God's help.

The God we serve is never far off; he enters into our perceived monotony, the daily rhythms of our lives, in order to make something extraordinary out of it all. Out of us. Moment by moment, day by day, year by year, God faithfully comforts our fears, tends our wounds, prepares our nourishment, and gives us opportunities to strengthen our muscle, our faith, our resolve. Through our parenting, God meets us in a fresh way, as a parent himself: a good, good Father, eager to love, to train, to encourage, and to bless. Through him we are seen and known and dearly loved. Because of him we are never alone. In him we are invited to grow up as children, as parents, as people.

I'll be honest: my patience still wears thin; my children continue to light up my life while also absolutely exhausting me beyond what seems reasonable for a couple of small humans. I haven't cracked the code of holiness; in fact, the longer I walk with Jesus, the more I learn that there are no recipes for success. There is only quiet, repeated faithfulness when we can, and rest in his presence when we are empty, since parenting empties us out more readily than most vocations possibly can. The secret to a sacred life is that there is no secret. Every day we come to God anew. Every day he meets us again. Fresh manna. Daily bread.

After pressing in more intentionally to these ancient spiritual practices, I find myself waking up to my days with new excitement and expectation, eager to see God at work in my littles, in my marriage, in my home, in my soul. When we seek the Lord, he will be found. When we have nothing left to give, he pours himself into us. As David Wright so sagely put it, "The light comes singing that the blind may learn to dance its dance as well."[115]

In this year, I've begun to learn this sacred dance: the call-and-response of the God who loves me, who meets me in the daily, mundane realities of parenthood, and who calls me further in to join in the great folk dance of grace with abandon, with joy. My steps are faltering ones, but I'm beginning to pick up on the rhythm.

Show up, take a step, follow the leader.

Love—trust—rest—repeat.

ACKNOWLEDGMENTS

To all the parents: this book is for you and because of you.

To my mom friends, too many to name, a dozen or so of whom show up in these pages. This journey would be utterly impossible—and *way* less fun—without you. Our calls, texts, playdates, coffee runs, rare and lovely nights out without our kids, and shared understanding that these years are both *so good* and *so hard* all at once buoy me up.

To my parents. Mom, I now know how hard you worked and how little you slept all those years. You survived raising three daughters with a smile, deeper love for Jesus, and a greater sense of humor to boot. You're an inspiration. Dad, you taught me that much of holy living boils down to telling the truth because it "is easier to remember" and going to bed when I'm tired because, as Vince Lombardi once said, "fatigue makes cowards of us all." Thank you both for your example of faithfulness.

To my sisters, Caitlyn and Caroline, moms both, who are teaching me that holiness and humility are part and parcel of parenting little people. Without you I'd be lost, and without all your hand-me-down maternity clothes I'd be naked.

To my church: thank you for walking alongside me as a mother in the faith, for modeling many of these spiritual disciplines, and for loving our little family so well.

To my writing cohorts—Grammatical Foibles, The Chapter, and For the Love—for your encouragement, cheerleading, and continued prayers. To my first readers—Alicia Akins and Bethany Rydmark—who managed to balance wise critique with honest feedback and abundant kindness. You are absolute gems.

To Dan Balow and the Steve Laube Literary Agency, and all the wonderful folks at Rose Publishing, especially Lynnette

Pennings and Kay ben-Avraham. Working alongside each of you has been a joy.

To Lincoln, Wilson, and Felicity, who made me a mom. You are the most delightful little people I've ever met, and you school me daily in holiness, tenderness, humor, and grace. Thank you for being such patient teachers.

And to Daryl, once again. I can't believe I get to live this life with you.

BIBLIOGRAPHY

Augustine. "Sermon, On Prayer and Fasting, LXXII." Quoted in Thomas Aquinas, *Summa Theologicae*. Public domain.

Baab, Lynne M. *Fasting: Spiritual Freedom Beyond Our Appetites*. Downers Grove, IL: InterVarsity Press, 2006.

Barclay, William. *A Barclay Prayer Book*. Louisville: Westminster John Knox, 2003.

Barton, Ruth Haley. *Sacred Rhythms*. Downers Grove, IL: InterVarsity Press, 2006.

Bauerlein, Mark, ed. *The Digital Divide*. New York: Penguin, 2011.

Bonhoeffer, Dietrich. "Learning to Die." *A Testament to Freedom*. New York: HarperOne, 1995.

———. *Life Together*. Minneapolis: Fortress, 2005.

———. *No Rusty Swords*. New York: Harper & Row, 1965.

Bowler, Kate. *Everything Happens for a Reason, and Other Lies I've Loved*. New York: Random House, 2018.

Breathnach, Sarah Ban. *The Simple Abundance Journal of Gratitude*. New York: Warner Books, 1996.

Browning, Elizabeth Barrett. "Sonnet 26." *Sonnets from the Portuguese and Other Poems*. New York: St. Martin's Press, 1986.

Brueggemann, Walter. *Awed to Heaven, Rooted in Earth*. Minneapolis: Augsburg Fortress, 2003.

Buechner, Frederick. *Peculiar Treasures*. New York: HarperCollins, 1979.

Cairns, Scott. *The End of Suffering*. Brewster, MA: Paraclete Press, 2010.

———. *Short Trip to the Edge*. Brewster, MA: Paraclete Press, 2016.

Calhoun, Adele Ahlberg. *Spiritual Disciplines Handbook*. Downers Grove, IL: InterVarsity Press, 2005.

Carretto, Carlo. *Letters from the Desert*. Maryknoll, NY: Orbis Books, 1972.

Chesterton, G. K. *A Short History of England*. CreateSpace Independent, 2016.

Crouch, Andy. *The Tech-Wise Family*. Grand Rapids: Baker Books, 2017.

David, Andrew, Tom Ryan, and Dan Rhodes, eds. "Prayer." *The Other Journal* 21 (April 2013): ix.

Dillard, Annie. *Pilgrim at Tinker Creek*. New York: HarperCollins, 1999.

Eckhart, Meister. "Sermon II: The Nearness of the Kingdom." *Meister Eckhart's Sermons*. London: Aeterna Press, 2015.

Foster, Richard. *A Celebration of Discipline.* New York: HarperCollins, 1998.

Foster, Richard, and Emilie Griffin, eds. *Spiritual Classics: Selected Readings on the Twelve Spiritual Disciplines.* New York: HarperOne, 2000.

Friedman, Edwin. *A Failure of Nerve: Leadership in the Age of the Quick Fix.* New York: Seabury, 2007.

Gaffigan, Jim. *Dad Is Fat.* New York: Three Rivers Press, 2013.

Gericke, Paul. *Crucial Experiences in the Life of D. L. Moody.* Chicago: Insight Press, 1978.

A Guide to Prayer for Ministers and Other Servants. Nashville: The Upper Room, 1983.

Hallesby, Ole. *Prayer.* Minneapolis: Augsburg, 1994.

Hamid, Mohsin. *Exit West.* New York: Riverhead Books, 2017.

Hare, Douglas R. A. *Matthew.* Interpretation. Louisville: Westminster John Knox, 1993.

Harper, Lisa Sharon. "Will Evangelicalism Surrender?" *Still Evangelical?*, edited by Mark Labberton. Downers Grove, IL: InterVarsity Press, 2018.

Hong, Edna. "A Look Inside." *Bread and Wine.* Walden, NY: Plough Publishing, 2003.

Kaling, Mindy. "The Dundies." *The Office*, Season 2, Episode 1, 2005. Directed by Greg Daniels. Aired 20 September 2005.

Keller, Timothy. *Walking with God through Pain and Suffering.* New York: Riverhead Books, 2003.

Kelly, Thomas R. *A Testament of Devotion.* New York: Harper, 1941.

Kenyon, Jane. "Let Evening Come." *Let Evening Come: Poems.* Minneapolis: Graywolf Press, 1990.

Lamott, Anne. *Hallelujah Anyway.* New York: Riverhead Books, 2017.

———. *Operating Instructions.* New York: Anchor Books, 2005.

———. *Traveling Mercies: Some Thoughts on Faith.* New York: Anchor Books, 1999.

Louf, André. *Teach Us to Pray.* London: Darton, Longman & Todd, 1974.

Lyall, Leslie T. *A Passion for the Impossible: The Continuing Story of the Mission Hudson Taylor Began.* London: OMF Books, 1965.

Marshall, Catherine. *A Closer Walk.* Ada, MI: Revell, 1986.

McEntyre, Marilyn Chandler. *A Faithful Farewell.* Grand Rapids: Eerdmans, 2015.

McKelvey, Douglas Kaine. "A Liturgy for Changing Diapers." *Every Moment Holy.* Nashville: Rabbit Room Press, 2017.

McNeil, Brenda Salter. *Roadmap to Reconciliation*. Downers Grove, IL: InterVarsity Press, 2015.

Milton, John. "On His Blindness." *The Complete Poems*. New York: Penguin, 1998.

Nee, Watchman. *The Normal Christian Life*. Carol Stream, IL: Tyndale House, 1977.

Newman, John Henry. *Parochial and Plain Sermons*. San Francisco: Ignatius, 1997.

Nouwen, Henri J. M. *Life of the Beloved: Spiritual Living in a Secular World*. New York: Crossroad, 1992.

O'Brien, Kevin. *The Ignatian Adventure*. New York: Crossroad, 1992.

Okoro, Enuma. *Silence and Other Surprising Invitations of Advent*. Nashville: Upper Room Books, 2012.

Oliver, Mary. "Maybe." *New and Selected Poems: Volume One*. Boston: Beacon Press, 1992.

Ortega, Fernando. "Traveler." *Storm*. World Records, 2002.

Peterson, Eugene H. *Eat This Book*. Grand Rapids: Eerdmans, 2006.

———. *A Long Obedience in the Same Direction*. Downers Grove, IL: InterVarsity Press, 2000.

Rahner, Karl. *Encounters with Silence*. South Bend, IN: St. Augustine Press, 1999.

Sleeping at Last. "One." *Atlas*. Asteroid B-612, 2017.

Stearns, Richard. *The Hole in Our Gospel*. Nashville: World Vision, 2014.

Steinbeck, John. *East of Eden*. New York: Penguin Books, 2002.

Stromberg, Bob. *Finding the Magnificent in Lower Mundane: Extraordinary Stories About an Ordinary Place*. Grand Rapids: Zondervan, 1994.

Taylor, Howard, and Geraldine Taylor. *Hudson Taylor's Spiritual Secret*. Chicago: Moody Publishers, 2009.

Van Loon, Michelle. *Born to Wander*. Chicago: Moody Publishers, 2018.

Varley, Henry. Quoted in Mark Fackler, "The World Has Yet to See…" *Christian History* 25 (1990). https://www.christianitytoday.com/history/issues/issue-25/world-has-yet-to-see.html.

Warren, Tish Harrison. *Liturgy of the Ordinary*. Downers Grove, IL: InterVarsity Press, 2016.

What about Bob? Directed by Frank Oz. Burbank, CA: Touchstone Pictures, 1991.

Wiederkehr, Macrina. *A Tree Full of Angels: Seeing the Holy in the Ordinary*. New York: HarperCollins, 1995.

Wilhoit, James C. *Spiritual Formation as if the Church Mattered*. Grand Rapids: Baker, 2008.

Willimon, William. "The God We Hardly Knew." *Watch for the Light*. Walden, NY: Plough Publishing, 2001.

Wilson-Hartgrove, Jonathan. *The Awakening of Hope*. Grand Rapids: Zondervan, 2012.

Wright, David. *Lines from the Provinces*. GreatUnpublished.com, 2000.

Wright, N. T. *After You Believe: Why Christian Character Matters*. New York: HarperOne, 2010.

———. *John for Everyone, Part 2: Chapters 11-21*. Louisville: Westminster John Knox, 2004.

———. *The Way of the Lord: Christian Pilgrimage Today*. Grand Rapids: Eerdmans, 1999.

NOTES

1   Leslie T. Lyall, *A Passion for the Impossible: The Continuing Story of the Mission Hudson Taylor Began* (London: OMF Books, 1965), 37.
2   Psalm 34:17 (MSG).
3   Adele Ahlberg Calhoun, *Spiritual Disciplines Handbook: Practices That Transform Us* (Downers Grove, IL: InterVarsity, 2005), 49.
4   Richard Foster, *A Celebration of Discipline* (New York: HarperCollins, 1998), 15.
5   Romans 13:14.
6   Calhoun, *Spiritual Disciplines Handbook*, 50.
7   Annie Dillard, *Pilgrim at Tinker Creek* (New York: HarperCollins, 1999), 10.
8   Romans 11:36 (ESV).
9   Watchman Nee, *The Normal Christian Life* (Carol Stream, IL: Tyndale House, 1977), 78.
10   N. T. Wright, *After You Believe: Why Christian Character Matters* (New York: HarperOne, 2010), 183.
11   N. T. Wright, *John for Everyone, Part 2: Chapters 11–21* (Louisville: Westminster John Knox, 2004), 74.
12   Foster, *Celebration of Discipline*, 126.
13   Ibid., 126–27.
14   Psalm 102:3a.
15   Psalm 119:84a.
16   Psalm 120:6.
17   Foster, *Celebration of Discipline*, 129.
18   William Barclay, *A Barclay Prayer Book* (Louisville: Westminster John Knox, 2003), 151.
19   Luke 22:26–27.
20   Edna Hong, "A Look Inside," *Bread and Wine* (Walden, NY: Plough, 2003), 25.
21   Karl Rahner, *Encounters with Silence* (South Bend, IN: St. Augustine Press, 1999), 48.
22   Matthew 11:28, Douay-Rheims Bible.
23   Psalm 127:2.
24   Kate Bowler, *Everything Happens for a Reason, and Other Lies I've Loved* (New York: Random House, 2018), 21.
25   Kevin O'Brien, *The Ignatian Adventure* (New York: Crossroad, 1992), 75.
26   Carlo Carretto, *Letters from the Desert* (Maryknoll, NY: Orbis Books, 1972), 161.
27   Calhoun, *Spiritual Disciplines Handbook*, 266.
28   Henri J. M. Nouwen, *Life of the Beloved: Spiritual Living in a Secular World* (New York: Crossroad, 1992), 76.
29   1 Thessalonians 5:17 (ESV).
30   Tish Harrison Warren, *Liturgy of the Ordinary* (Downers Grove, IL: InterVarsity Press, 2016), 40.

31   Psalm 85:8 (NLT).

32   Andrew David, Tom Ryan, and Dan Rhodes, eds., "Prayer,", *The Other Journal* 21 (April 2013): ix.

33   Ole Hallesby, *Prayer* (Minneapolis: Augsburg, 1994), 18.

34   Scott Cairns, *Short Trip to the Edge* (Brewster, MA: Paraclete Press, 2016), 114.

35   André Louf, "Teach Us to Pray," *Spiritual Classics: Selected Readings on the Twelve Spiritual Disciplines*, ed. Richard Foster and Emilie Griffin (New York: HarperOne, 2000), 33.

36   Dietrich Bonhoeffer, *Life Together* (Minneapolis: Fortress, 2005), 92.

37   Luke 6:21 (RSV).

38   Douglas R. A. Hare, *Matthew*, Interpretation (Louisville: Westminster John Knox, 1993), 38.

39   Macrina Wiederkehr, *A Tree Full of Angels: Seeing the Holy in the Ordinary* (New York: HarperCollins, 1995), 53.

40   Lisa Sharon Harper, "Will Evangelicalism Surrender?" *Still Evangelical?*, ed. Mark Labberton (Downers Grove, IL: InterVarsity Press, 2018), 30.

41   *What about Bob?*, directed by Frank Oz, 1991.

42   John Steinbeck, *East of Eden* (New York: Penguin Books, 2002), 520.

43   Matthew 23:23.

44   Bowler, *Everything Happens for a Reason*, 38.

45   Eugene Peterson, *Eat This Book* (Grand Rapids: Eerdmans, 2006), 4.

46   Howard Taylor and Geraldine Taylor, *Hudson Taylor's Spiritual Secret* (Chicago: Moody Publishers, 2009), 223.

47   Marc Prensky, "Do They Really Think Differently?" *The Digital Divide* (New York: Penguin, 2011), 13.

48   Nicholas Carr, "Is Google Making Us Stupid?" *The Digital Divide* (New York: Penguin, 2011), 33–35.

49   Carretto, *Letters from the Desert*, 96.

50   Bianca Bosker, "The Binge Breaker," *The Atlantic*, November 2016, https://www.theatlantic.com /magazine/archive/2016/11/the-binge -breaker/501122/.

51   Matthew 6:16–17.

52   Lynne M. Baab, *Fasting: Spiritual Freedom Beyond Our Appetites* (Downers Grove, IL: InterVarsity Press, 2006), 106.

53   Exodus 19:15.

54   Daniel 10:3.

55   Baab, *Fasting*, 107.

56   Catherine Marshall, *A Closer Walk*, excerpt reprinted in "A Fasting on Criticalness," *Renovaré*, 16 May 2018, https://renovare.org/articles/a-fasting -on-criticalness.

57   Jean M. Twenge, "Have Smartphones Destroyed a Generation?" *The Atlantic*, September 2017.

58   Foster, *Celebration of Discipline*, 56.

59   2 Peter 2:19.

60   Basil the Great, "First Homily on Fasting," translated by Kent Burghuis, Orthodox Christian Campus Ministries, Rutgers University, http://rutgersnb.occministries.org/wp-content/uploads/2015/07/St.-Basil -the-Great%E2%80%99s-First-Homily-on-Fasting.pdf, accessed 7 July 2018.

61   Andy Crouch, *The Tech-Wise Family* (Grand Rapids: Baker Books, 2017), 41.

62   Scott Cairns, *The End of Suffering* (Brewster, MA: Paraclete Press, 2010), ix.

63   Bowler, *Everything Happens for a Reason*, 49.

64   Timothy Keller, *Walking with God through Pain and Suffering* (New York: Riverhead Books, 2003), 190–91.

65   François Fénelon, *A Guide to Prayer for Ministers and Other Servants* (Nashville: The Upper Room, 1983), 344.

66   John Milton, "On His Blindness," *The Complete Poems* (New York: Penguin, 1998).

67   Marilyn Chandler McEntyre, *A Faithful Farewell* (Grand Rapids: Eerdmans, 2015), 23–24.

68   Henry Varley, quoted in Mark Fackler, "The World Has Yet to See … " *Christian History* 25 (1990), https://www.christianitytoday.com/history/issues /issue-25/world-has-yet-to-see.html.

69   William Willimon, "The God We Hardly Knew," *Watch for the Light* (Walden, NY: Plough Publishing, 2001), 148.

70   Thomas R. Kelly, *A Testament of Devotion* (New York: Harper, 1941), 33.

71   Erica Goode, "Study Finds TV Alters Fiji Girls' View of Body," *The New York Times,* May 20, 1999, https://www.nytimes.com/1999/05/20/world/study -finds-tv-alters-fiji-girls-view-of-body.html.

72   Calhoun, *Spiritual Disciplines Handbook*, 31.

73   Ruth Haley Barton, *Sacred Rhythms* (Downers Grove, IL: InterVarsity Press, 2006), 12.

74   Calhoun, *Spiritual Disciplines Handbook*, 32.

75   G. K. Chesterton, *A Brief History of England* (CreateSpace Independent, 2016), 36.

76   Anne Lamott, *Traveling Mercies: Some Thoughts on Faith* (New York: Anchor Books, 1999), 272.

77   Meister Eckhart, "Sermon II: The Nearness of the Kingdom," *Meister Eckhart's Sermons* (London: Aeterna Press, 2015), 8.

78   Karl Barth, quoted in Bob Stromberg, *Finding the Magnificent in Lower Mundane: Extraordinary Stories About An Ordinary Place* (Grand Rapids: Zondervan, 1994), 69.

79   Sarah Ban Breathnach, *The Simple Abundance Journal of Gratitude* (New York: Warner Books, 1996), 2.

80   Genesis 12:1; Exodus 3:10; 1 Kings 18:1.

81   Jonah 1:2.

82   Luke 2:27.

83 Matthew 2:13.

84 Michelle Van Loon, *Born to Wander* (Chicago: Moody Publishers, 2018), 14.

85 N. T. Wright, *The Way of the Lord: Christian Pilgrimage Today* (Grand Rapids: Eerdmans, 1999), 13.

86 Matthew 8:20.

87 Luke 9:3.

88 John 3:8 (RSV).

89 Acts 16:6.

90 Van Loon, *Born to Wander*, 74.

91 1 Corinthians 13:4 (NKJV).

92 James 1:19.

93 Nicole Nordeman, Twitter post, 7 July 2018, https://twitter.com /nicholenordeman/status/1015563547559030785.

94 Anne Lamott, *Hallelujah Anyway* (New York: Riverhead Books, 2017), 7.

95 Carretto, *Letters from the Desert*, 22–23.

96 Mary Oliver, "Maybe" *New and Selected Poems: Volume One* (Boston: Beacon Press, 1992), 97.

97 Willimon, "The God We Hardly Knew," 149.

98 Anne Lamott, *Operating Instructions* (New York: Anchor Books, 2005), 113.

99 Proverbs 3:12.

100 Fernando Ortega, "Traveler," *Storm*, World Records, 2002.

101 Matthew 16:24.

102 John Henry Newman, *Parochial and Plain Sermons* (San Francisco, CA: Ignatius, 1997), 1712.

103 Leviticus 23:1–2.

104 "The Dundies," *The Office*, Season 2, Episode 1, 2005.

105 Sleeping at Last, "One," *Atlas*, Asteroid B-612, 2017.

106 Dietrich Bonhoeffer, "Learning to Die," *A Testament to Freedom* (New York: HarperOne, 1995), 265.

107 Revelation 19:9 (ESV).

108 Barton, *Sacred Rhythms,* 13.

109 Edwin Friedman, *A Failure of Nerve: Leadership in the Age of the Quick Fix* (New York: Seabury, 2007), 63–64.

110 1 Corinthians 13:1.

111 Cairns, *Short Trip to the Edge*, 128.

112 Thomas More, "A Godly Meditation," *Spiritual Classics*, 6.

113 Elizabeth Barrett Browning, "Sonnet 26," *Sonnets from the Portuguese and Other Poems* (New York: St. Martin's Press, 1986), 17 (gender inclusive language mine).

114 Douglas Kaine McKelvey, "A Liturgy for Changing Diapers," *Every Moment Holy* (Nashville: Rabbit Room Press, 2017), 55.

115 David Wright, "Lenten Preludes," *Lines from the Provinces* (GreatUnpublished. com, 2000) 14.

ALSO BY COURTNEY ELLIS

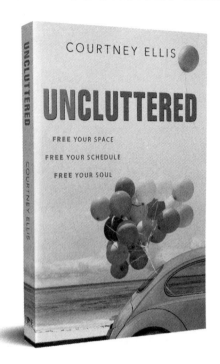

"Peace. Less. Still. Enough. Simple. Clear. Rested. Read Uncluttered."
— JOHN ORTBERG

Too much stuff. Too many activities. Too much exhaustion. Too much stress. How can we sift through the busyness, the mess, and the stress to uncover the abundant life God offers? In *Uncluttered*, one woman shares her journey from a life of stress, stuff, and burnout to one of peace, space, and fulfillment. You'll learn tips for paring down your possessions, simplifying your schedule, and practicing the ancient art of Sabbath.

Uncluttered is not a formula about what "stuff" you need to give up. It's about slowing down long enough for God to remind you of his truth and what it means to be his child.

ISBN-13: 9781628627916

www.hendricksonrose.com